Family
PHOTO
Detective

Family PHOTO Detective

Learn How to Find **GENEALOGY CLUES** in Old Photos
and Solve **FAMILY PHOTO MYSTERIES**

MAUREEN A. TAYLOR

FAMILY
TREE
BOOKS
Cincinnati, Ohio
shopfamilytree.com

Contents

"The likeness is called a good one,
I believe, though, if the family proverb
be true, it must be a very ugly picture.
My claim to pre-eminent 'homeliness'
has never been disputed."

—LETTER FROM ISAAC NEWTON CUSHMAN TO HENRY WYLES CUSHMAN, 1854. FROM THE CUSHMAN COLLECTION, NEW ENGLAND HISTORIC GENEALOGICAL SOCIETY

Introduction

JONATHAN GALLI

On winter afternoons during my childhood, my sister and I would sit with our mother and talk about the last fifty years of our family history, using photographs as the inspiration for the stories. I would spend hours imagining what life was really like for the people in the pictures and searching their faces for family resemblances. Whom did my sister resemble? Was it true that almost everyone had blue eyes? Our ancestors stared at us from faded photographs, captured for eternity by a camera. The images never changed, but our questions about them did. As we grew older our inquiries became more sophisticated, leading to richer, more detailed stories.

By paying attention to the details in the images, we were able to find clues to the identity and character of the people in the portraits. In some cases there was a photographer's imprint; in others, a handwritten scrawl on the back identifying the person as "Aunt Loretta." Pictures alone, however, couldn't give us the full story behind the images. To fill in the gaps, we needed the family history.

Genealogists are used to examining documents, asking questions, and researching data. These same skills enable you to decipher the clues in a family portrait. Basic questions such as who is depicted and who is not, what their clothes tell us, or where and with whom are they posed can help you break down a brick wall in your family research.

While examining your family photographs may initially raise more questions than answers, patience and persistence can solve the picture puzzles in your family album. Start by constructing a list of questions about each family photograph. If the photo is a formal portrait, you may wonder why they chose the props pictured. Other questions to ponder: Did the people change their appearance for the photographer? Did he or she adopt a new hairstyle, or remove a pair of glasses? Can you tell how they felt about being photographed? Do the pose and expression tell anything about the individual? If you look closely, questions will be raised whose answers can shed light on the life, times, and personalities of your ancestors.

WHAT IS A FAMILY PHOTOGRAPH COLLECTION?

A family photograph collection is more than a random assortment of images—each picture is a time capsule that documents a moment from the lives of our ancestors. The collection may contain formal portraits, snapshots of vacations, relatives gathered for special events, friends, and pets. These photos show you what was important to your ancestors. Each image is full of information, but a collection of photographs arranged and identified can tell the story of a lifetime or the history of a family.

The images are documentation of our ancestors' lives. They provide clues for further genealogical research or furnish material not found in any standard genealogical resource. However, photographs tell only part of the story. To fully research your ancestors, you have to look at all the documents created in their lifetime. Only then will you have a complete "picture" of the people who came before you. When visual and written materials are combined in a family history, a wonderful story emerges.

Think about the many moments you immortalize with photos. It's difficult to find a household today without a camera, yet to our ancestors, picture-taking was a new endeavor. Photography changed the way people thought about themselves and the world. The family photo collection became a valuable possession for many reasons, but one of the biggest is that photos contain a record of the past. Pictures of family milestones or people who have passed away are treasured for the memories they invoke and the legacy they can pass on.

When you gather all your family photographs together from their various storage places, you may be

COLLECTION OF THE AUTHOR

Family photos provide genealogists with visual clues about the lives of their ancestors.

Do you know who the photographer in your family was?

if given an opportunity. After making sure that all the members of my family were safe, I would grab my small collection of photographs. They are my family's collective memory—my children's first steps, riding without training wheels, and birthday parties. It is also the only record in my possession of my grandparents. The only grandparent I ever knew lives in those pictures and connects me with the past.

ABOUT THIS BOOK

For many individuals, the anonymous faces that stare back from shoeboxes and albums tucked away in the attic or closet are interesting but puzzling. This book will enable you to discover the visual heritage of your family by evaluating and understanding the various aspects of the photographs in your possession. It will assist you in your quest to find out more about your relatives by explaining how to identify the different types of photos, research the photographer, and date the costumes. You will learn how to compare images for facial characteristics. Each chapter contains charts and illustrations to guide you through the process. Case studies provide examples of how other people have solved their photographic mysteries.

The photographs that appear in this book were selected on the basis of their visual value. The majority were purchased for use in this publication and are not identified. The sight of all these unidentified images for sale at auctions has inspired me to write this book. Our family photographs are too valuable to become someone else's "instant ancestors."

Any images used in the case studies are primarily from the collections of friends and family and have been identified using the techniques described in this book.

HOW TO USE IT

The purpose of this book is to assist you with the identification and interpretation of your family images. It will:

- function as a reference tool (bibliographies, charts, and worksheets).
- define and illustrate the process of photo identification.
- explain the steps in identifying and dating a family photograph.
- expand your skills to include the resources particular to photo research.

surprised by their diversity. If your family collection dates from the beginning of photography (1839–1840), you'll have a wide variety of photographic examples from several generations—more than 150 years of family photo history. The pictorial documentation of ancestral lives is vast. Spread out a group of the images and study the panorama of your family's visual history. It forms a timeline. You can watch a baby grow to old age as the photographic process changes. It is the history of the births, loves, and deaths of our ancestors.

Studio portraits of immaculately dressed and posed family members allow us to view our ancestors from a certain distance, while snapshots involve us in their lives. Candid shots provide us with an opportunity to see our ancestors at play, at work, and at home. By researching family photographs, you can gain a better understanding of the everyday lives of your ancestors and a precious glimpse into their personalities.

A close friend of mine lost everything she owned in a fire. This caused me to reflect on what I would save

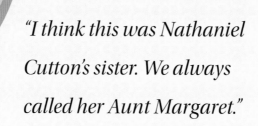

"I think this was Nathaniel Cutton's sister. We always called her Aunt Margaret."

—ANONYMOUS, FROM THE BACK OF A PHOTOGRAPH

1

Bringing the Past to Life

When was the last time you looked at your family photographs? If you haven't taken them out of their storage place recently, now is the time. One of the first steps in compiling a genealogy is to examine all possible sources of information in your home. Photographs are a valuable resource for family historians.

c. 400 B.C.
Chinese philosopher Mo-Ti formally records the creation of an inverted image formed by light rays passing through a pinhole into a darkened room.

1727
Professor J. Schulze discovers that light darkens silver nitrate. This becomes the basis of photographic processes.

1800
Thomas Wedgwood makes the first photograms using natural objects on leather and paper coated with silver nitrate.

1816
Joseph Nicéphore Niépce uses the camera obscura to produce images on photosensitive paper; ten years later he creates a permanent image.

1839
William Henry Fox Talbot announces his paper photographic process to the Royal Society of London.

A family photograph collection is a direct link to your past. Family history is, after all, about the individuals in these photographs, and images can bring the past to life and provide insights into the lives of our ancestors. Photographs show who attended weddings, birthday celebrations, and other important family events. They may provide you with a sense of your ancestor's personality. Every photograph of Uncle Charlie may show him clowning for the camera while Aunt Minnie smiles demurely.

Photographs can even unite families. Genealogists in the same family may share research and discover that their photo collections contain copies of the same images. The unidentified photos in your collection may have names and dates in a relative's. You may have an unidentified photograph of a young child, while a distant relative has not only the child's name, but several photographs of that same individual at different ages. Connecting with family enriches your genealogical research and can even expand your collection of family pictures.

COMPILING A VISUAL HISTORY

As genealogists, it is important for us to compile the visual history of our families as well as the written information. Documents provide data, but pictures show you the past.

Each image contains a series of clues that can assist you with your research. A photographer's imprint may reveal the places where your ancestor lived, or an artifact depicted in an image may be something you own today. By closely examining a picture, you may spot a chair that

COLLECTION OF THE AUTHOR

Photographers often took multiple portraits in one sitting, circa 1908.

matches one in your house. Photographs can give you clues to the previous owner of an object, clues that might not appear in probate documents or other records.

Clothing clues can date images, establish ethnic connections, and reveal personality. Images of ancestors dressed in attire from a particular country provide evidence of their immigrant roots and fascinating details about their native culture. You may even discover an ancestor's political or social viewpoints through an image. For instance, your great-great grandmother might be wearing the pants-like bloomers adopted by early dress reform advocates Amelia Bloomer and Elizabeth Cady Stanton, while men's lapels might sport buttons endorsing presidential candidates. Interpreting costume details is a key part of understanding and dating family photos.

Photos, even identified ones, raise questions about your family. Why was grandfather wearing that costume? Where are all the children in the group photograph? Using your skills as a genealogist, you may be able to answer those questions and bring new meaning to your family album.

Family photograph collections are as diverse as families themselves—their composition and size depends, in part, on geography and economic status. If a family lived in a rural area that lacked a photographer's studio, there might not be any portraits of them. Affluent families enjoyed photography as a recreational pursuit, while urban, working-class families had little time or money for such things. The photographic record of your family depends on the variables of interest, economics, place of settlement, access to a photographer or equipment, and even religious affiliation. Some religions, such as the Society of Friends (Quakers), originally discouraged members from having photographs taken. If your ancestors were part of a religious group that discouraged photography, your collection may be smaller. When looking at the photographs in your possession, remember to think about your family in the context in which they lived.

One of the contributing factors to the size of a family collection was the novelty of photography in the nineteenth century. In your collection, you may have several different types of images of one ancestor taken around the same time. Photographers advertised the newest techniques and styles of photographs—method, content, and purpose changed often—to entice customers

COLLECTION OF THE AUTHOR

Photographers lured customers into their studio by advertising their skills. This poster dates from Christmas 1897.

to return to their studios. Our ancestors, as consumers, sought the latest trend or new technique in order to capture the best representation of themselves.

Technological limitations, however, influenced the quantity and content of photos. For instance, all photographs in the early nineteenth century were taken under natural light. Artificial lighting wasn't available until the 1880s. The limits of the early equipment also influenced the type of image that could be taken. A basic

GENERAL GUIDELINES

1. Handle photographs carefully.

2. Use a worksheet to record data.

3. Develop a research strategy.

4. Cite your sources.

5. Be persistent.

understanding of photographic methods used in the past can provide background and additional hints in your investigation of your family photographs.

Evaluating, dating, and identifying a photograph is a multistep process. Determining the method of photography, researching the photographer, appraising the costume, and verifying the genealogical information are all important steps toward solving your photo mystery. Along the way, you'll consult experts and conduct library research. The process can be time-consuming, but very rewarding.

To get started, you must develop a new way of looking at photographs—the smallest detail can yield an important clue or the answer to a family mystery. A family

KEY TO GROUP PORTRAIT SHOWN

Include name and life dates for each individual.

1. *Ellen Derry Stone*

2. *Alberta Davis (1912-1996)*

3.

4. *Miss Meagher (school teacher)*

5.

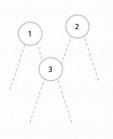

A key similar to the one shown helps to keep track of the ancestors in this photo.

TOOLS OF THE TRADE

There are a few basic tools that assist with the investigative process.

Magnifying Glass or Photographer's Loupe

Noticing the smallest details can help you solve a picture riddle. Look for tiny clues with a magnifying glass (any kind will do) or a photographer's loupe, a small magnifying device that professional photographers use. You can purchase magnifying glasses at any office supply store, drugstore, or chain store such as Wal-Mart. To buy a loupe, try the local camera shop; prices range from less than ten dollars to more than fifty.

Cotton or Nonlatex (and Powder-Free) Medical Examination Gloves

No matter how clean you think your hands are, each time you handle your photographs without wearing lint-free cotton gloves or nonlatex ones, you leave behind a little bit of dirt and oil. You can find cotton gloves in some hardware stores, but I prefer to buy multiple pairs from specialty suppliers. Examination gloves are available at warehouse stores and at pharmacies. Wash the cotton gloves after use and dispose of the nonlatex ones. See the appendix for a list of suppliers.

Measuring Tape

A measuring tape with both inches and centimeters allows you to compare your images to size charts that can help you determine what photographic method was used to take the picture.

Pens and Pencils for Marking Images

As long as you write on the back of your images using the right pencil or pen, you shouldn't cause any damage. When identifying heritage photographs, use soft lead pencils, such as the graphite ones used by artists. Pens for writing on plastic-coated prints need to be quick-drying, permanent, and odorless when dry. Check their packaging to see if writing implements are photo-safe.

Protective Sleeves, Photo Albums, and Storage Containers

Look for acid- and lignin-free pages and plastic overlays made from polypropylene a non polyvinyl chloride plastic (PVC) or other inert plastic. Stay away from albums with magnetic pages that contain adhesive—it can damage your images. The best albums also have slipcases that protect pages from dust. Storage boxes should be made of the same materials as albums and have reinforced corners.

Scanner

Scanners are great photo identification tools—they enable you to enlarge features in photographs, copy images, and upload pictures to the Web to share with relatives. Some have capabilities for scanning negatives and slides. Before you purchase a scanner, make sure it's compatible with your existing computer equipment, read reviews, and ask friends. You can enlarge or reduce photographs once you've scanned them at a minimum of 600 dpi color and at least 100 percent scale. It's advisable to save your images as tif files, an uncompressed image format.

Worksheets

Record your research, measurements, and observations on one of the worksheets in the appendix to keep track of your data.

heirloom, such as a piece of jewelry, might enable you to identify a person in a photograph. A sign in the background or a photographer's studio prop can help date an image. You will need to scrutinize each photograph closely to itemize all the particulars.

HOW TO GET STARTED

Family photo research requires developing a research strategy, keeping good records, and having patience. Picture researchers and genealogists use a wide variety of sources to solve a problem, and one of the primary rules of genealogy and photo research is to cite those sources. Citations validate the information found and provide a reference point for further research. If your resources are properly cited, anyone could pick up your research and know exactly where you got what.

Rules to Follow

Break your picture research project down into segments that can be worked on one at a time. It's easier to piece together the history of an image and draw conclusions regarding the identity of the events, persons, or family members depicted if you work on only one photograph at a time.

Examine Your Family Photographs

With your own photographs it may be difficult to notice what clues exist because you've looked at them so many times. The first step in working with your family photographs is to pretend you've never seen them before. Find the clues using a magnifying glass or scanner to enlarge sections. Move across the picture in a methodical pattern, carefully examining each person in the image from head to toe, as well as the background.

Use a Worksheet

Note everything you discover, but don't add up all your clues until you've finished your research. Use a worksheet (sample sheets are located in the Appendices) to record your findings and citations. Carry the worksheets and copies of the images with you on research trips. Attach a photocopy of the image to the worksheet to keep the photo on hand without damaging or losing the original.

Group portraits require a modification of the worksheet. In addition to attaching a photocopy, making a sketch of a group photo can serve as a key to the details in the image. Assign a number to each person in a group image to help with identification and recording information (see the Key to Group Portrait Shown sidebar).

MAKING COPIES OF PHOTOS

Whether you want to make copies for research purposes or duplicate photographs in a relative's collection, you'll want to explore the options.

- Use your digital camera to make a copy. With a steady hand or a tripod, you can take digital images of original photographs.

- When you take film negatives to be developed, order an extra set of prints or a CD (to make copies at home).

- Make a copy using a self-operated machine like Kodak's Picture Kiosk. It allows you to crop, enlarge, reduce red-eye, and add creative borders. You can make prints that range from wallet size to 8" × 12", or you can download the picture to a disk.

- Use a scanner. With scanners available for less than one hundred dollars, there is no reason not to own one. Most come with editing software and some have tutorials that lead you through the process. You can scan photographs, negatives, and even slides.

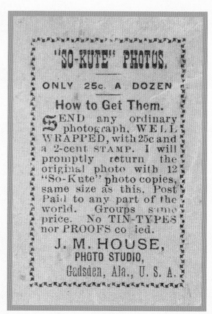

COLLECTION OF THE AUTHOR

TITLE/SUBJECT/CAPTION: *[Alice McDuff]*

IDENTIFYING MARKS: *photographers imprint on lower right*

PHOTOGRAPHER'S NAME: *Jean L. Harbeck,*

Pawtucket City Directories 1903–1940

COLORING DETAILS: *None*

COSTUME DESCRIPTION: *Fitted dress with large buttons*

wearing watch and locket

OTHER INFORMATION:

OWNER'S NAME: *Maureen Taylor*

ADDRESS:

TELEPHONE NUMBER:

CONDITION: *Excellent*

TYPE OF IMAGE: *photo print*   SIZE (H X W): *5″ × 3.5″*

MOUNTED?   YES (NO)   THICKNESS:

ORIGINAL OR COPY? *original*

PHOTOGRAPHER'S IMPRINT: *Harbeck-Pawtucket*

DATES OF OPERATION: *1903–1940*

PROPS/BACKGROUND: *props—bench, bannister*

background—painted backdrop with columns

COSTUME TIME FRAME: *1910–1916*

WHEREABOUTS OF NEGATIVE: *unknown*

Develop a Research Plan

There are four steps involved in developing a successful research plan:

1. Use a worksheet to help you set your research priorities and keep track of what you've accomplished and what you still need to do.
2. Contact relatives early in the identification process who may be able to identify some of the individuals in a group portrait or suggest a date for an event.
3. Genealogical research provides you with materials to further identify the photograph—family papers, census records, and newspapers can place a photograph within a time frame.
4. At some point, it's likely only a library will have the resources you need to answer specific questions. Books, manuscripts, and online resources can provide direction when you seem to run out of ideas.

IDENTIFICATION TIPS

There are many things that can help you determine the identity of the mysterious people in your family photos; several different types of clues exist. While not all family photographs will have the photographer's name and address—which is one of the best and most revealing pieces of information—more general clues, like photographic method and costume, can help you date the picture.

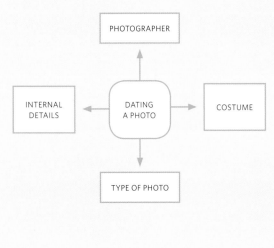

WAYS TO DATE A PHOTOGRAPH

PHOTOGRAPHER

INTERNAL DETAILS ← DATING A PHOTO → COSTUME

TYPE OF PHOTO

WHAT DO YOU DO IF YOU CAN'T IDENTIFY A PHOTO?

- Show the picture to as many relatives as possible. You don't know when someone will have an identical copy they've already identified.

- Post it on a Web site, yours or someone else's. A number of sites (listed in chapter six) help to identify photographs or reconnect people with lost family photographs.

- Advertise your family on a message board or query column. While you can't add a photograph to your message or query, you can verbally describe the picture and ask for help.

- Reexamine your genealogical data. Were any relatives living in the area where the photograph was taken?

Photographic Method

One of your first steps should be to try to determine the date of the image by the technique used to take the picture. Each method or style of photography has identifiable characteristics. By comparing the image in question to a chart of stylistic differences, a range of dates can be determined. (See chapters three, four, and five.)

Internal Details—Props, Background, and Facial Characteristics

Details in the picture that you may have initially missed will become apparent under close examination. Props, backdrops, and signage, for example, can help identify when and where an image was taken. Facial characteristics can also assist in the identification process. (See chapter eight.)

Photographer's Name

If the photographer is identified, you can determine when he was in business, which can help assign a specific date and location to an image. These are important facts for your genealogical research. (See chapter six.)

The process of solving a photographic mystery is dependent on your knowledge of family history, as well as a variety of identifying clues. It isn't always possible to put a name to a face—there will always be times when missing pieces of genealogical information or insufficient evidence in the photograph will work against you—but you won't know that until you start examining the picture and researching its clues. It's important to follow a series of photo identification steps and develop new ways of looking at pictures.

Seeing the Evidence: Family History

Barbara DiMunno thinks that either her great aunt Lillian (Clark) Hewitt (1873–1955) or Lillian's mother Harriet (Ogden) Clark (1842–1912) originally owned the photo to the right. She is trying to verify a time frame for the image so she can work on identifying the people depicted.

Type of Photograph

Different types of photographs existed in the nineteenth century, including shiny metal daguerreotypes (1839–c.1860), glass ambrotypes (1854–c.1870), iron pictures called tintypes (1856–twentieth century), and paper photographs (1850–today). In the twentieth century, the majority of images taken were paper. In this example, the picture is a paper print. Unfortunate, because it doesn't help narrow the timeframe.

Photographer's Imprint

Many nineteenth- and early twentieth-century photos contain the name of the photographers as well as the town where they operated their studios. Using city directories and directories of photographers working in specific areas, you can usually determine a span of dates for when the photo was taken. Unfortunately, there is no photographer's imprint on this picture, but the presence of a photographer's white backdrop, foliage, and dirt in the foreground confirms that this image was taken outdoors, probably by an itinerant photographer. This could mean that the family lived in a rural area that was visited by a traveling photographer.

BARBARA DIMUNNO

Internal Clues: Personality, Clothing, and People

The major person in the photograph is the mother, and her personality is apparent in the way she dominates the image with her stance. With one hand on her hip and the other on the photographer's chair, she draws attention to her tiny waist which was no doubt held in place by a restrictive corset commonly worn in the nineteenth and early twentieth century. The fact that she wears such an undergarment is a costume clue. According to Beatrice Fontanel in *Support and Seduction: The History of Corsets and Bras* (New York: Harry Abrams, 1997), these undergarments were popular from the 1870s through 1914. This provides a tentative time frame for the image. This mother followed the late nineteenth- and early twentieth-century fashion ideal of having a waist small enough that her husband's hands could touch while encircling it.

CASE STUDY continued next page →

A costume encyclopedia, like John Peacock's *20th Century Fashion* (London: Thames & Hudson, 1993), indicates that the mother's dress with the full collar and sleeves resembles dresses worn circa 1906. The deep V-neck opening, white high-necked shirt, and tight lower sleeves with fullness at the upper arms are also characteristic of that period. This clothing information suggests the picture was taken between 1900 and 1910. A ten-year timeframe allows for stylistic variations.

An infant is the next subject in this family photograph. Let's hope this picture was taken in warm weather, since the baby is naked upon a folded handmade quilt. It was and still is common to photograph an infant without clothes to show off its perfection. If you look closely, you'll see a pair of hands holding the baby at the waist. A woman's skirt is visible underneath the chair. There is no clue as to her identity. It is also difficult to tell if the baby is male or female. Finding a child born between 1900 and 1910 in genealogical data could identify the whole family.

The three girls in this photograph are wearing dresses of similar design and fabric and lockets. The four children appear to be about two years apart in age. The younger of the girls on the right is standing very still with one hand on the chair. The oldest child wears her hair in a topknot much like her mother. Girls' attire mimicked women's fashions. She appears to be holding something in her hands, but what it might be isn't clear. That she is leaning toward her younger sister perhaps suggests that the girls have a close relationship.

It isn't apparent what was happening off-camera to capture the attention of the children. While the mother is looking directly into the camera, all the children are glancing off to the side of the photographer. Very likely, an assistant was attracting their attention with a toy. As every parent knows, nothing is more difficult to capture on film than an active child. These four children are very well-behaved for their age, and it was probably a combination of a mother's strict warning and the actions of the assistant that made for a successful portrait.

Drawing a Conclusion

The final step in photo identification is adding up all the clues to develop a conclusion. In this case, the mother's costume provided a time frame, yet even with a date for the photograph, Barbara DiMunno is unable to name the family in this portrait. While Lillian (Clark) Hewitt (1873–1955) would be the right age for the woman in this portrait, other pictures of her confirm that she is not the mother pictured. By using observation and research, Barbara DiMunno now knows a lot more about this photograph, even though she can't name the subjects.

Try applying these techniques to your photographs and see if you can uncover new family history or an interesting story. You might be surprised by what you discover.

Costume

The clothing worn by the people in the picture can provide a wealth of information. Identifying the style of clothing in an image is crucial to dating the photograph. Women's clothing, in particular, can be broken down into distinct features that can place an image within a time frame. (See chapter nine.)

DRAW CONCLUSIONS

If you follow this advice, you will gain a better understanding of the images in your collection, the types of photographs you have, and approximate dates for each. In the best cases, you will develop feasible conclusions about the identity of the individuals in the photographs. When you've added up all the clues, start by determining a reasonable date for the photo; follow that with a tentative guess at the identity of the people pictured and prove that with genealogical research and family help.

If your first attempts at research are unsuccessful, put the photograph aside and work on another. The information you find during research on another image may provide solutions to the first.

Screenshot of Flickr

If you want to take a sneak peek at photo collections from other families try Flickr **<www.flickr.com>**. Individuals, museums, and archives upload pictures to this website to share them with others. It's like a picture wiki. You can comment on images to help identify them, take a visual walk through history and, if the Flickr contributor allows, you can even download photos.

On Flickr, anyone who posts images is called a contact. Finding new contacts is easy. First, sign up for a Flickr account following the instructions on the homepage. Basic Flickr use is free, but if you want unlimited uploads, there is a pro-level membership offered for $24.95 a year.

After you've signed up, click on Contacts (located in the top menu), then select "Find your friends" in the drop-down menu. This will help you find individuals and organizations (or other genealogists) that participate on the site. Use the search box on the bottom of the screen to search for organizations or keywords to locate appropriate Flickr pages.

Click the link to look at their Flickr page, known as a photostream, then click Profile. You'll learn more about the organization, usage rights and when they joined Flickr. In some cases, along the right-hand side of the page, you'll see a list of other collections (groups of images) that this contact has uploaded. Add an organization or individual to your contact list so you can see when they add new images to their photostreams.

Some Flickr streams you may want to follow are:

United States National Archives <www.flickr. com/photos/usnationalarchives>: has a Flickr page and uses collections and sets. For instance, I was looking for images of women so I clicked on Collection, then selected one called "women's history." Doing that led me to subsets of images so that I could look at images from World War II or "Women in Mathew Brady pictures." Selecting the Mathew Brady subset directed me to a page with a short overview of the collection and thumbnails of the images. Click on any one of those small images takes to you a page for that image, which contains information on copyright, and any caption info. Right click on the image to see different downloadable versions of it.

Library of Congress <www.flickr.com/photos/ library_of_congress>: There are plenty of photos to view on the LOC page, but there is also a collection of Illustrated Newspaper Supplements from the *New York Tribune*. It's a fascinating group of covers from the *New York Tribune* beginning in 1909. The LOC is using crowd-sourcing to help solve their unidentified photo mysteries. For instance, in their collection "Mystery Photos solved" they asked Flickr users to annotate twenty-two unidentified travel scenes. Within days, they had their answers.

George Eastman House <www.flickr.com/ photos/george_eastman_house>: This photostream isn't the largest collection of online images, but it provides an overview of the history of photography from daguerreotypes to a lovely group of autochromes (colored images from the early twentieth century).

National Archives of the United Kingdom <www.flickr.com/photos/nationalarchives>: Here you can view historic or contemporary images or narrow your selection by using the menu under the main title. "Collections" (in the menu bar) lets you see specific images arranged by group while "sets" organizes them into smaller categories. "Archives" allows you to select images by the date they were taken or when they were uploaded to Flickr. You can time travel to the United Kingdom through nine hundred years worth of material in their archive.

Library of Canada <www.flickr.com/photos/ lac-bac>: The Library and Archives of Canada post behind the scenes images of their museums, but they don't stop there. You can also view items from their collections.

Charlie

Leo

Ecio

Dino

Louis

Aunt.

"Looking at family photographs makes you remember people and events you had forgotten."

—Interview with James W. Taylor Jr.,
18 January 1999

2

Talking with Relatives

Family history is the sum of the information that exists in your family's old documents, photographs, and memories. Talking with relatives is a necessary part of any family research, but it becomes more important when photographs are involved. A picture can trigger remembrances of past events that result in new family data. In addition, there's always the chance that family members will know the names of the people in your pictures and the stories behind the photographs.

1845
The first genealogical society in the world, the New England Historic Genealogical Society, is founded in the United States.

1930s
Federal Writers from the Works Progress Administration begin tape recording the life stories of more than ten thousand men and women from a variety of regions, occupations, and ethnic groups.

1894
The Family History Library of the Church of Jesus Christ of Latter-day Saints opens in Salt Lake City, Utah, and begins collecting genealogical material and assisting members with their research.

1996
Ancestry.com becomes the first family history Web site to publish the Social Security Death Index and other large databases online.

The process of collecting verbal memories through interviewing is called oral history, and it's the cornerstone of all genealogical research. Make the most of your interviewing visit, e-mail, or letter by following these steps.

THE INTERVIEW PROCESS

The first step in an oral history interview is locating family members that have a sense of family history and can recall it. Older members of a family tend to have the oldest and most interesting stories, but younger relatives with more reliable memories can sometimes be the most helpful. You should show the image you are trying to date and interpret to more than one relative. Everyone remembers an event differently; one person might retain certain details, while someone else has a completely different interpretation of the event.

An elderly relative may remember all the names of the people in the portrait and may also have a story about the day the picture was taken. A friend's aunt told her about what it had been like to travel to the city to sit for a family portrait. She recalled that she had never seen a tin ceiling before and couldn't take her eyes away from it. Her story explained why she was looking up in the family portrait. Her aunt also identified everyone in the picture, but it was her story that enriched the family history.

When showing a photograph to relatives, prepare a list of questions prior to your visit. The photograph will dictate the type of questions you ask. The details that appear in the image may lead to other avenues of inquiry. For example, one woman I know had a box of family photographs that were taken before she was born. She showed them to her much older siblings to find out when and where they were taken. During the course of the interview, the siblings began referring to each other using nicknames. She was amazed—since her siblings only used them to communicate among themselves, she had never been aware of these nicknames. Her brothers and sisters shared with her the origins of those nicknames and why they used them. A whole new understanding of her immediate family was uncovered in one afternoon by looking at family photographs.

Jackie Hufschmid is one determined genealogist. It took three years, but she finally identified the young couple in this family photograph. You can duplicate her success by following these three steps to solve your own picture puzzles.

1. Add Up All the Photographic Evidence

Type of Photograph: Mounted on a card 4½" × 6 ½", this portrait is an example of a cabinet card. Introduced in 1866, cabinet cards were popular into the early twentieth century.

Photographer's Imprint: The photographer, Bonell, chose to place his imprint on the front of the card. By consulting Carl Mautz's *Biographies of Western Photographers* (Brownsville, Calif.: Carl Mautz Publishing, 1997), I learned that Bonnell worked in Eau Claire and Chippewa Falls, Wisconsin, from 1875 to 1890. This information provided Hufschmid with a fifteen-year timeframe for the image.

Fashion Details: Clothing clues provided a more specific date. The woman's dress has tight lower sleeves and high puffed shoulders, which were in style circa 1890. By 1893, sleeves were fuller on the upper arm. The skirt has a scalloped edge, which was trendy in the late 1880s. The woman's hairstyle—center part, short frizzed bangs, and a bun at the nape of her neck—also dates to the late 1880s. Her husband's clothing, a black sack suit with a buttoned vest, white shirt, and silk tie was fashionable during the same period. All of their costume details confirm that the picture dates from circa 1890.

2. Network

An amazing thing happened when the photograph appeared online as part of the "Identifying Photos" feature on the *Family Tree Magazine* Web site. The magazine received several e-mails from people who said that they had seen the photograph before. A couple of people even owned a copy! Months later, when the picture accompanied an article in *Family Tree Magazine*, a few more people contacted the magazine seeking additional information on the photograph. A network of family historians developed, and they worked together to find a common ancestor and

JACKIE HUFSCHMID

JACKIE HUFSCHMID

identify the image. Still, it would take three more years to put names to these faces.

3. Re-Evaluate Your Research

After learning where the picture was taken, Hufschmid re-examined her genealogical research to try to find a connection to Eau Claire, Wisconsin. Although she knew her family had lived in Wisconsin, she couldn't link

CASE STUDY continued next page →

her relatives specifically to Eau Claire. Hufschmid also double-checked all her family photographs just in case she had overlooked other evidence. In spite of her efforts, the image remained a mystery.

Last summer, Hufschmid and her father visited a cousin in Wisconsin. The conversation turned to family history and she mentioned her photographic brick wall. Her cousin revealed that two of their female relatives had moved to Eau Claire in the late 1800s—one to open a dress shop and the other to work in it. Eureka! There was the connection.

Once she had names and a link to Eau Claire, Hufschmid realized she owned another picture of the couple taken at a later date—a photo she had eliminated because of the missing Eau Claire information. Once home, she placed the identified 1920s image of the couple and their children next to the original portrait of the young couple, and she knew she had a match. The mystery people were Julia Gullickson (1872-1948) and her husband, James Wood (1868-1933). Scanning and enlarging sections of the image to compare facial features confirmed the identification.

This single image unlocked a piece of family history—but only because Jackie Hufschmid refused to give up. A final piece of the puzzle still remains, though: How does this photo connect all the people that came forward after seeing it? Given her resources and tenacity, Hufschmid is sure to find out.

Help With Captions

Relatives can also help you decipher mysterious captions that appear on photographs. Captions may include only partial names or nicknames of the people depicted. These can refer to "Aunt Eliza," or "Polly," or tell you that the photograph was a gift "From Tante to Fredy." Learning just one missing surname from a relative can open many genealogical doors; you may be able to match family resemblances or time periods to link other photos with the one they've identified.

Occasionally, you may get lucky and discover a photo with a thorough caption. More complete captions may include the date the picture was taken and the life dates of the person depicted. On the back of one unidentified photograph in my collection (not family) is written "Dear Sister Harriet born Febr. 16, 1840—Lee Cor, Penna, Franklin T.P. died Reunion Cor. Penna Oct. 1865 New Hope T.P."

Until the genealogical research is complete, there is no proof that the people in your photo collection are members of your family. They could be friends, schoolmates, or co-workers of your ancestors. The back of another unidentified photo of mine says: "My best girlfriend who I went to school with." This caption eliminates the girl depicted from consideration as a family member.

SAMPLE INTERVIEW QUESTIONS

Do you recognize this photograph?

Are any of the people in the photograph familiar?

Who are they and how do you know them/how are you related to them?

Was this picture taken for a particular occasion?

Does this photograph remind you of any family events or stories?

Who owned the photograph before you?

Do you have a collection of family photographs?

COLLECTION OF THE AUTHOR

In this casual group portrait, several Bessette family members and at least one unidentified individual are shown. When the photograph was shown to an older family member, she explained that this was a picture of her parents and her oldest sibling as a toddler. She assumed that the unidentified, taller adult woman must be a boarder, since her family operated a boardinghouse. The two older children were cousins living with them at the time.

According to the narrator, the young child in the image was her older sister Loretta, who was born 25 November 1916, to Eugene Joseph Bessette and his wife Alice (McDuff), who are also in the photo. The older children are Dolores and Pete, children of Albert McDuff, the brother of Alice. They were supposedly living with the Bessettes because their mother had died.

Census records verify the name of the parents and the baby, but do not identify the name of the unknown person or prove that Pete and Dolores were living with the couple. City directories provided an address for the family, but do not offer evidence that the family operated a boardinghouse. Family folklore and passenger lists confirm that the family traveled between the United States and Canada to visit relatives. In fact, the Bessettes' first child, Loretta, was born in Canada.

By consulting genealogical data on the McDuff family, it was possible to contact a sibling of Pete and Dolores from their father's second marriage. He filled in a few missing pieces. His father, Albert McDuff, lived with his parents for several years so that they could help him care for his two children after the death of his first wife. Pete and Dolores never lived with the Bessettes, according to their younger sibling. Alice (McDuff) Bessette, as the youngest member of the McDuff household, was also living at home at the time her brother lived there with the two children. She helped her parents care for the children.

While it was not possible to verify the unknown person in the photo or the boardinghouse story, research was able to help verify visual family information presented in the image. In this case, oral history interviews helped us interpret the image. They provided the details of the story and the names of the primary subjects. Without this information, it would have been difficult to research the image. While the oral history interviews did not answer all the questions raised by the photo, they supported the genealogical research.

In a friend's collection is an image with an extensive caption on the back written in a foreign language. Relatives identified the woman in the image but were unable to translate the message. The owner of this photograph was hopeful that it would reveal family information. When translated, it stated that this was a picture of the woman's new business. She had just opened it and was proud of her accomplishment—specifically mentioning her new telephone. Without the caption, the information in the image would be a puzzle.

Ask About Other Photographs

The solution to your photo mystery may be a shoebox away. While asking relatives to identify pictures in your collection, don't miss an opportunity to look at their boxes of images. The unidentified image in your hands could have a caption in their family album. Relatives may also own documents or other materials that can lead to an identification.

Follow-Up Later

Take a good-quality photocopy of the image with you to leave with your relatives. They may want to review the photograph again later. Also, consider conducting a follow-up visit—it can lead to more discoveries. After showing a relative a few photographs of an ancestor, one family learned of some documents in a distant relative's possession that pertained to the photos and had become separated from the images over a few generations.

PHOTOGRAPHS AS MEMORY TRIGGERS

COLLECTION OF THE AUTHOR, CIRCA 1934

Never underestimate the power of a single photo. You can use a picture to unlock a person's memory. The sight of a single image can help a person recall the moment the photo was taken, and it can also lead to stories worth recording. This simple image is of a young girl with her two older sisters. The girl is my mother. When I showed her this image, she told me how her eldest sister and her sister's future husband used to like to buy her pretty clothes and take her to the movies. She couldn't recall when this image was taken, but when I asked if she remembered anything else, she shared a great tale about her first day of kindergarten and memories of all those movies. Now I know why she loves films— they bring back memories of her family connection.

Every photo in my box of family photographs triggered related memories. It's possible to tell your family story one picture at a time.

No doubt about it, Michael R. Boyce has spent a lot of time working on his family history. He's discovered that some of the stories his father told him appear to be true, such as being related to a Dutch sea captain. He's also uncovered photographs of many family members who have lived since the advent of photography in 1839. As with all family history research since the explosion of interest in Internet genealogy, there are those unexpected moments and uncanny connections you make online that help you unravel mysteries. In Michael's case, not only did he find a name change, but an eastern link to his ancestor Stephen V. Boyce and additional photographs.

Michael Boyce had heard that a member of his family was from the eastern United States, but couldn't discover any information linking his great-great-grandfather Stephen V. Boyce to other Boyce families. A response to a posting on an online message board solved the puzzle. It turned out that Stephen was the son of John Boice and had run away from home, eventually ending up on the West Coast and settling on San Juan Island in Washington state as Stephen Boyce rather than Boice. Michael thinks that this tintype is a picture of Stephen's father John. Name change is not unusual in this family—the name apparently derives from a Dutch name, Buys, and appears with different spellings in various documents.

John Boice was born in 1794 in Columbia County, New York, and died 4 July 1876, in Greene County, New York. According to federal census records, he was a farmer until a few years before his death. Michael thinks this portrait is John, his third-great-grandfather, because he has photographs of two of John's three brothers (Eli, Jacob, and William). He thinks William died sometime around the mid-nineteenth century. Since this picture is of a man in his later years, it couldn't be William. Only John is left as a possible identification. So is this a picture of John Boice?

The answer is perhaps. There is no identifying information on the photograph to connect this image to John. It was, however, provided by a cousin who also had pictures of the other two brothers. Unfortunately, this type of photograph doesn't provide a narrow timeframe. Tintypes were introduced in 1856 and, in some places, are still available today.

Clothing clues usually help determine a date for an image, and in this case, the man is wearing work clothes suggestive of the 1860s. In the 1860s, John Boice would have been in his sixties and still working his farm. There is striking evidence of the hard life of a farmer present in this picture. Take a look at the hand leaning on the arm of the chair. Both his middle and little fingers have bruised fingernails and he is missing the first joint of his index finger. He also appears to have something wrong with his right eye. Since there is no way to prove or disprove the identification at this point, it very well could be John Boice.

MICHAEL BOYCE

Unidentified group, 1840s.

"If our children and children's children to-the third and fourth generation are not in posses-sion of portraits of their ancestors, it will be no fault of the Daguerreotypists of-the present day; for verily, they are limning faces at a rate that promises soon to make every man's home a Daguerrean Gallery. From little Bess, the baby, up to great-great-grandpa, all must now have their likenesses; and even the sober [Quaker], who heretofore rejected all the vacuities of portrait-taking, is tempted to sit-in the operator's chair…"

—T. S. ARTHUR, "AMERICAN CHARACTERISTICS: THE DAGUERREOTYPIST," *GODEY'S LADY'S BOOK*, 38, MAY 1849

3

Cased Images
Daguerreotypes, Ambrotypes, and Tintypes

The very first photographs our ancestors saw amazed them. They marveled over the intricacy and minute detail of these earliest images. We live in such a visually oriented world it's impossible to imagine what it must have been like for our forebears to see a photograph for the first time. Our ancestors embraced photography and fell in love with its qualities. The demand for the new images spurred inventors to develop new and cheaper ways to produce photographs.

1839
A patent is issued to Frenchman Louis Daguerre for a method of capturing images on metal.

1850
The 1850 Census lists 938 males over the age of fifteen with the occupation of daguerreotypist.

1856
Tintype introduced by Hamilton L. Smith of Ohio.

1840
The first daguerreotype studio opens in New York City.

1854
James Ambrose Cutting is issued a patent for the ambrotype.

The progression from the first photographs to contemporary digital photography is an interesting history. It is a topic genealogists need to understand in order to correctly and thoroughly interpret their photograph collections. Identifying the type of photo you are looking at is the first step in the process of evaluating and interpreting your family's visual heritage. It is part of setting your family into the historical context in which they lived.

DAGUERREOTYPES

Daguerreotypes, the first photographic images, are small metal photographs with reflective surfaces. Invented by Frenchman Louis Daguerre in 1839, daguerreotypes were more affordable than painted portraits, but not as flattering. The clarity and truthfulness of the images awed our ancestors. Daguerreotypes became known as "mirrors with a memory." A popular 1850s children's story included the following quote from a grandmother who had just received some daguerreotypes from her grandchildren.

I'm so happy! I keep them where I can look at them all the time, with the cases open, that your bright faces may be looking upon me constantly; and at night, when I go

COLLECTION OF THE AUTHOR

Daguerreotype of boy, 1850s.

to bed, I stand them open on the table side of me, where they may be the first things I shall see, as I open my eyes in the morning.

The earliest daguerreotypes were still-life subjects—it took almost five minutes to create the image. However, once the exposure time decreased, the majority of daguerreotypes were portraits. The major flaw of the new invention was that it required technical skill and artistic talent in order to capture a good image. Individuals look stiff and uncomfortable in daguerreotypes, and quite possibly, they were. There is debate over whether their expressions were a reflection of the seriousness of sitting for a photograph or if they were uncomfortable due to the braces used to hold them still.

Daguerreotypists also used implements and tricks to assure a flattering image. Head braces attached to chair

DAGUERREOTYPE PLATE SIZES	
Imperial/ Mammoth plate	Larger than 6 ½" × 8 ½"
Whole plate	6 ½" × 8 ½"
Half plate	4 ¼" × 5 ½"
Quarter plate	3 ¼" × 4 ¼"
Sixth plate	2 ¾" × 3 ¼"
Ninth plate	2" × 2"
Sixteenth plate	1 ⅜" × 1 ⅝"

Daguerreotype in pieces.

backs helped individuals hold their head still for the required amount of time. Standing braces held people by the head, neck, and waist. The smallest movement could blur the portrait. Wax was used to fix ears that stuck out and cotton could be used to puff up hollow looking cheeks. The best images were those that were well lit and well composed. Each cased daguerreotype consists of the metal image, a mat that frames the image, a cover glass, edging known as "the preserver" because it holds all the parts together, and a case.

Despite their quality issues, daguerreotypes were very popular. Between 1840 and 1844, daguerreotypists in the United States took more than three million images. New industries to manufacture the metal plates and cases developed. Within a year of the daguerreotype's invention, studios operated in all the major cities

DAGUERREOTYPE BIBLIOGRAPHY

America and the Daguerreotype, edited by John Wood (Iowa City: University of Iowa Press, 1991).

American Daguerreian Art by Floyd and Marion Rinhart (New York: Clarkson N. Potter, 1967).

The American Daguerreotype by Floyd and Marion Rinhart (Athens: University of Georgia Press, 1981).

American Daguerreotypes: From the Matthew R. Isenburg Collection by Richard S. Field and Robin Jaffee Frank. (New Haven, Conn.: Yale University, 1989).

The Daguerreian Annual. (Pittsburgh: The Daguerreian Society, issued annually).

The Daguerreotype in America by Beaumont Newhall (New York: Duell, Sloan & Pearce, 1961: reprint New York: Dover Publications, Inc. 1976).

The Daguerreotype: Nineteenth Century Technology and Modern Science by M. Susan Barger and William B. White (Washington, D.C.: Smithsonian Institution Press, 1991).

Mirror Image: The Influence of the Daguerreotype on American Society by Richard Rudisill (Albuquerque, N.M.: University of New Mexico Press, 1971).

The Scenic Daguerreotype: Romanticism & Early Photography by John Wood (Iowa City: University of Iowa Press, 1995).

Secrets of the Dark Chamber: The Art of the American Daguerreotype by Merry A. Foresta and John Wood (Washington: National Museum of American Art, Smithsonian Institution Press, 1995).

THE DAGUERREOTYPIST (EXCERPT)

Godey's Lady's Book, May 1849

If our children and children's children to the third and fourth generation are not in possession of portraits of their ancestors, it will be no fault of the Daguerreotypists of the present day; for, verily, they are limning faces at a rate that promises soon to make every man's house a Daguerrean Gallery. From little Bess, the baby, up to great great-grandpa', all must now have their likenesses; and even the sober Friend, who heretofore rejected all the vanities of portrait-taking, is tempted to sit in the operator's chair, and quick as thought, his features are caught and fixed by a sunbeam. In our great cities, a Daguerreotypist is to be found in almost every square; and there is scarcely a county in any state that has not one or more of these industrious individuals busy at work in catching "the shadow" ere the "substance fade." A few years ago it was not every man who could afford a likeness of himself, his wife or his children; these were luxuries known to those only who had money to spare; now it is hard to find the man who has not gone through the " operator's" hands from once to half-a-dozen times, or who has not the shadowy faces of his wife and children done up in purple morocco and velvet, together or singly, among his household treasures. Truly the sunbeam art is a most wonderful one, and the public feel it is a great benefit!

If a painter's studio is a place in which to get glimpses of human nature, how much more so the Daguerreotypist's operating-room, where dozens come daily, and are finished off in a sitting of half a minute. Scenes ludicrous, amusing or pathetic, are constantly occurring. People come for their portraits who have never seen the operation, and who have not the most distant conception of how the thing is done. Some, in taking their places in the chair, get so nervous that they tremble like aspens; and others, in the vain attempt to keep their features composed, distort them so much that they are frightened at their own image when it is placed in their hands.

It is often a matter of surprise to some that two portraits of the same person by different Daguerreotypists should appear so unlike, it being supposed, at first thought, that nothing more than mechanical skill was required in the individual managing the instrument, and that it was only necessary for the image of

THE DAGUERREOTYPIST.

The Daguerreotypist (excerpt)
Godey's Lady's Book, May 1849

the face to enter the lens and impress itself upon the chemically prepared plate, to have a correct likeness; but this is an error. Unless the Daguerreotypist be an artist, or have the educated eye of an artist, he cannot take good pictures, except by the merest accident; for, unless the sitter be so placed as to throw the shadow on his face in a certain relation to his prominent features, a distortion will appear, and the picture, therefore, fail to give satisfaction. The painter can soften the shadows on the face of his sitter so as to make them only serve the purpose for which he uses them, but the Daguerreotype exercises no discrimination, and reflects the sitter just as he presents himself. It was owing to bad positions and bad management of light that the earlier Daguerreotypists made such strange-looking pictures of faces, one side of which would be a dark shadow and the other a white surface, in which features were scarcely distinguishable. But great improvements have taken place, and some establishments are turning out pictures of remarkable beauty and excellence.

In order to obtain a good picture, it is necessary to go to a Daguerreotypist who has the eye and taste of an artist, or who employs such a person in his establishment; and it is also necessary to dress in colors that do not reflect too much light. For a lady, a, good dress is of some dark or figured material. White, pink or light blue must be avoided. Lace work, or a scarf or shawl sometimes adds much to the beauty of the picture. A gentleman should wear a dark vest and cravat. For children, a plaid or dark-striped or figured dress is preferred by most Daguerreotypists. Light dresses are in all cases to be avoided.

of the eastern United States, and itinerants brought the medium to the smaller towns. Studios displayed sample portraits so prospective customers could judge the quality of their work. Daguerreotypists in larger cities like New York had elaborate sitting rooms and furnishings. Comfortable surroundings allowed patrons to relax before having their picture taken.

A visit to the daguerreotypist's studio required patience and preparation. Studios and popular magazines published guides on dressing for the camera. *Godey's Lady's Book*, a nineteenth-century woman's magazine, advised dressing in dark or patterned fabric that would not reflect too much light. White, pink, and light blue were to be avoided, while lacework or a scarf or shawl added to the picture. A dark vest and cravat were the recommended dress for men. Children dressed similar to adults in plaid or dark striped dresses. If a person showed up for a sitting without the necessary accoutrements, the studio would often supply props, shawls, lace collars, and even jewelry to enhance the portrait.

Daguerreotypists came from a variety of occupational backgrounds. Some were painters and others merely wanted to augment their regular livelihood. For instance, G.G. Walker of Providence, Rhode Island, took daguerreotypes and sold musical instruments.

AMBROTYPES

It was not long before people became dissatisfied with the daguerreotype. It was expensive and required long sittings, and the end result was difficult to view. In the mid-1850s, a new type of image appeared—the ambrotype. Instead of a metal surface, ambrotypes were made with a piece of glass coated with light-sensitive collodion, a mixture of ether and guncotton.

Each ambrotype portrait consisted of the glass image, a dark backing, a mat, a cover glass, a preserver, and a case. Most ambrotypes were backed with either black velvet or paper to make the negative image a positive. A coating of black varnish could also be used to save money. The black backing brings the portrait into focus. When the image is removed from its backing, the detail of the image is lost.

There are a few similarities between a daguerreotype and an ambrotype. Each image was a unique copy. Only a single ambrotype or daguerreotype could be produced at a time. If an individual wanted other copies of a

Ambrotype in pieces.

portrait, additional photographs had to be taken. Ambrotypes were available in the same sizes as daguerreotypes, since photographers used the same cases for both. The most popular sizes were the sixth and quarter plate. Also, the image typically appears reversed in both ambrotypes and daguerreotypes—details appear as they would in a mirror. Some photographers solved this by flipping over the ambrotype and facing the collodion side out.

By 1856 the ambrotype was enjoying a short-lived period of popularity. While the daguerreotype required a certain amount of training to obtain a good impression, ambrotypists could easily learn how to capture an image. They were also cheaper to produce than daguerreotypes and did not have to be viewed in a special light, but they were extremely fragile.

TINTYPES

In 1856, an Ohio chemistry professor named Hamilton L. Smith patented the process of coating an iron plate with light-sensitive chemicals. The iron was then coated with a black or brown varnish. The resulting image was a direct positive when viewed on the dark background. These images were known as melainotypes or ferrotypes, because of the iron backing. They were also called

COLLECTION OF THE AUTHOR

Tintypes are photographs on metal. This image contains the outline of a scalloped mask from when it was stored in a case, 1860s

DON'T CLEAN THEM YOURSELF!

Individuals with cased images in their collection are often tempted to clean a cased image themselves. This can irreparably damage the image. What looks like dirt on the glass could be a problem with the image itself. It is best to leave the restoration work to professional conservators. A list of conservators appears in the appendix.

Daguerreotypes consist of several different layers: the metal plate, the mat, the cover glass, the edging to hold the parts together, and the case that they're placed into. These images are inherently fragile. The salts on the metal plate can be wiped away or the plate scratched, permanently obscuring or damaging the image.

Daguerreotypes will often exhibit a type of haze on the glass or a halo around the image. It is difficult

for an untrained individual to ascertain the cause of the damage and how to prevent further deterioration.

There are two reasons why ambrotypes are fragile: They are made on glass and the image is a coating on the surface of the glass. Any attempt to clean the surface will either damage or destroy the image. Over time, the collodion can lift away from the glass surface and flake off.

Tintypes are somewhat more durable, as the collodion, a light-sensitive photographic chemical, is coated on a metal plate. However, when exposed to moisture, the iron will rust and any type of surface abrasion will remove or scratch the image.

With these cautions in mind, the best rule to follow is: Leave all restoration to a professional.

CASED IMAGES CHARACTERISTICS		
Daguerreotype	**Ambrotype**	**Tintype**
Mirror-like surface	Negative on glass	Negative on iron
	Appears as a positive image	Appears as a positive image
Must be held at an angle to be seen	Backed with a dark background	Fixed on a black metal background
Usually cased	Usually cased	Paper mat or case
1839	1854	1856

tintypes because of the use of tin shears to cut the photographs out of the iron sheet.

The iron tintypes were more durable and weighed less than daguerreotypes and ambrotypes. They did not scratch as easily as daguerreotypes or break like ambrotypes. Tintypes could be carried in a pocket or sent through the mail without risk. A coating of clear varnish further protected the image.

Most photographic improvements prior to the tintype had been developed in Europe. The tintype, however, is an American invention—it was the first photographic format patented by an American. Tintypes remained in use from 1856 until the mid-1930s.

Tintypes were fast and cheap to produce. A customer could walk into a studio, sit for a portrait, and walk out in as little as ten minutes with multiple copies. The speed with which a picture could be taken led the process to be referred to as "instantaneous." An image could cost as little as a few cents.

These inexpensive images were commonly found on the frontier, in small towns, and in working-class urban districts. Individuals who were previously unable to afford a portrait could now obtain one. The images were acceptable, even though they had a cold, dull appearance and all the whites appeared gray.

New applications drove the popularity of these iron images. The election of 1860 pioneered campaign buttons made of tintypes with presidential candidates on them. The Civil War also helped. Traveling photographers often accompanied military units and set up shop where they camped. The low cost of the image allowed even the poorest soldier access to an image he could send home to his family. By the twentieth century, vacationers returned home from resorts carrying tintypes.

At first, only one image could be produced at a time, but once cameras with multiple lenses appeared, identical portraits could be produced in one sitting. Individuals could now obtain myriad copies of their portraits to give to friends and family. The number of lenses on the camera limited the number of copies produced.

Tintypes appeared in many of the same image sizes as daguerreotypes and ambrotypes. The size of a sheet of iron and the type of camera limited the maximum size to 10" × 14". The smallest images were approximately an inch square. These tiny images were called "gems" or "thumbnails" and could be kept in special tintype albums that fit in the palm of a hand. Since tintypes were approximately the same size as daguerreotypes and

TINTYPE SIZES (IN CASES)	
Whole plate	6½" × 8½"
Half plate	4½" × 5½"
Quarter plate	3¼" × 4¼"
Sixth plate	2¾" × 3¼"
Ninth plate	2" × 2½"
Sixteenth plate	1⅜" × 1⅝"
Gem or thumbnail	¾" × 1" (or smaller)

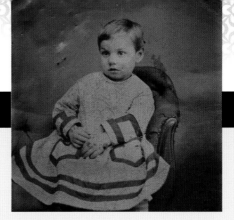

MEGHAN ROBERTS

What's the most common type of photograph found in family collections other than paper images? Tintypes! These curious genealogical gems appear in most family photo collections for three reasons: They were cheap, quick to produce, and durable. They also have a surprising longevity that has helped them survive for generations. Also called ferrotypes or melainotypes, tintypes came in several different styles and sizes. With almost a hundred years worth of tintypes in family collections, dating them can be tough. Six clues to look for when identifying your mystery tintypes are:

1. Cases. As with daguerreotypes and ambrotypes, photographers sealed early tintypes in cases.

2. Paper sleeves. Many tintypes were placed in paper sleeves rather than cases. You can usually pick out images created during the Civil War because their sleeves were often embossed with stars and other patriotic symbols.

3. Size. Pictures came in a variety of sizes (see "Tintype Sizes" sidebar).

4. Revenue stamps. Turn over your tintype to see if a revenue stamp is visible. Between 1 Aug. 1864 and 1 Aug. 1866, the U.S. government levied a tax on photos. Photographers had to affix a stamp to the backs of their images and hand-cancel each stamp with their names or initials and the dates of sale. That date can help you compile a list of ancestors who lived in the right place and time. See chapter four for more on revenue stamps.

5. Clothing. Tintypes are usually found without a case, paper sleeve, or revenue stamp, so we must rely on clothing clues to date them.

6. Family information. Adding up the photographic clues is just part of the process of identifying an image. You also need to consult your genealogical research. Clothing, cases, and other clues can provide a tentative date for the picture, but your family history research can definitively put a name with a face.

Applying the Process
Meghan Roberts found this tintype in her grandparents' trunk of old family photos. The tintype doesn't have a case, paper sleeve, or revenue stamp, so Roberts must rely on size and clothing clues to estimate when the picture was taken. Here's how the evidence stacks up:

• At 2⅜" × 3½", this tintype is an example of a bon ton, popular from 1865 to about 1910.

• Although the child is wearing a dress, we know that he's a boy because his hair is parted on the side. Boys and girls wore similar clothing until about age five, so it's not unusual to find boy toddlers in dresses. The style of his clothing—the boots and the wide trim on the dress—was common in the mid-1860s and early 1870s. This is a difficult image to date because the clothing lacks accessories that could narrow the time frame even further.

• Roberts thinks this is a portrait of someone in the Weekly/Weekley family because most of the other photographs in the collection are from that family. She thinks it could be her great-grandfather, Marion Lester Weekly, who was born in 1875.

• The more clues in a family picture, the more likely you are to identify the subject. In Roberts' case, we have only three clues to help identify the image—the image's size, the clothing clues, and family information. The size of the plate tells us that the image was taken after the mid-1860s. And although the clothing appears to date from the late 1860s, the mother may have dressed her son in outdated or modified styles because of economic circumstances. Unless Roberts has another child in her family tree that fits the age of the toddler in this portrait, it's reasonable to assume that the boy could be Marion Weekly. Additional family research could turn up other identified portraits of Weekly as a child and confirm the identity.

Tintypes are remarkable pieces of family history because they withstand abuse. Even when bent, rusted, and darkened from age, these pocket-sized treasures are well worth the identification effort.

ambrotypes, frugal photographers could place them in the presentation cases previously used to house the other types of photos. They could also be placed in paper mats produced exclusively for tintypes.

Most tintypes are a brown or chocolate color. Collectors claim that tintypes were also manufactured in a variety of other colors, including blue and yellow, but these are extremely rare.

HOW TO IDENTIFY A CASED IMAGE

The chart "Cased Image Characteristics" on page 37 describes the distinguishing features of each type of image commonly found in cases. The most difficult to differentiate are the ambrotype and tintype because of the similarity of their appearance when in a case.

Sometimes part of the backing is missing and negative qualities are visible, which clearly classifies the image as an ambrotype. In instances where this is not apparent, you can carefully remove an image from its case using a small suction cup. Be careful not to damage the case itself in the process.

Daguerreotypes are easily identified because of their reflective surfaces. However, you will find misidentified images for sale by individuals not familiar with the differences.

DATING A CASED IMAGE

Because of their fragility, early photographs required a case. The four pieces of a standard cased image were the image itself, a cover glass, a mat, and a preserver to hold the unit together.

Case Construction

The basic materials used in cases in the 1840s were wood frames and embossed leather. The clasp was typically a hook and eye. Inside the case was a velvet pad. The velvet, which could be red, purple, or green, could be embossed with the photographer's name and address.

Papier-mâché cases were also popular in the 1840s. They could be waterproofed with a variety of substances, such as sulphate of iron, quicklime, glue, or egg whites. They could also be made fireproof with borax and phosphate of soda. The decorative features of the cases were enhanced with inlaid mother of pearl.

In 1854, Samuel Peck patented the new, more durable thermoplastic case known as a union case. In some publications, authors mistakenly refer to these "union cases" as being composed of gutta-percha, an early plastic. They were actually composed of gum shellac, woody fibers, or other fibrous material and had several advantages over the old cases. They could be molded to hold any surface design, were dyeable, and were available in a variety of shapes. Most of the cases remaining today are black or brown, but they were also manufactured in red, green, tan, and orange.

All cases, regardless of their composition, were manufactured in standard sizes to accommodate the average sizes of the images. There was a slight variation between manufacturers in the outside dimensions.

Case manufacturers were generally not identified, with the exception of the photos of Mathew Brady and John Plumbe Jr. Before the appearance of manufactured cases, photographers built their own.

STANDARD CASE STYLES	
Style	**Average Size**
Whole	7" × 9"
Half	5" × 6"
Quarter	4" × 5"
Sixth	3½" × 3¾"
Ninth	2½" × 3
Sixteenth	2" × 2"

Other than its construction, one of the best ways to date a case is through surface design. Initially, case designs were based on Greek and Roman forms, such as the lyre. In the 1840s, nature subjects were popular, such as fruits, birds, marine life, and flowers. The rose motif had at least thirty variations from 1844 to 1850.

The intricate designs of the union case allowed artists to create works based on famous paintings. The increase in Catholic immigration to the United States popularized Christian religious scenes prior to the Civil War. Nationalistic themes increased during the Civil War. Photographic trends also influenced case design. The availability of post-mortem photography gave rise to themes related to death. Home scenes depicting domestic bliss, such as couples playing chess or other family scenes, were also common.

Just as case designs changed over time, so did the brass mats that framed the cased images. Mats came in several different styles such as fire-gilt, engraved, stamped, or common. Acids were applied to the surface, making the appearance frosted, marked, pebble, or sand finished. The mats were then lacquered. In the 1840s, the octagon shape was popular. In the 1850s, mat designs became more elaborate. Popular styles were elliptical, nonpareil, double elliptical, ornate elliptical, oval, and ornate border.

Each book in the Dating Cased Images sidebar outlines when particular cases were popular and who manufactured them. *American Miniature Case Art* includes biographies of the case makers and engravers. It also has charts of the case sizes offered by various manufacturers. You can date a case by comparing it to the illustrations and charts in these reference books.

Liners sat inside each case across from the image and came in various colors and designs, some of which include the name of the photographer. Use Adele Kenny's book to date the velvet liners.

FACTORS TO CONSIDER WHEN DATING A CASED IMAGE

- Photographer's imprints: Daguerreotypists often followed the custom of painters and "signed" their work by scratching their names into the metal plate.

- Photographer's name on the brass mat or velvet interior of the case.

- Composition of case.

- Design on surface of case.

- Hinges.

- Mat shape and style.

DATING CASED IMAGES

Consult these excellent guidebooks to help you date the pieces of a case:

American Miniature Case Art by Floyd and Marion Rinhart (South Brunswick, N.Y.: A.S. Barnes and Co., 1969).

Nineteenth Century Photographic Cases and Wall Frames by Paul K. Berg (2d ed.: Paul K. Berg, 2003).

Photographic Cases: Victorian Design Sources, 1840–1870 by Adele Kenny (Atglen, Pa.: Schiffer, 2001).

Union Cases: A Collector's Guide to the Art of America's First Plastics by Clifford and Michele Krainik with Carl Walvoord (Grantsburg, Wis.: Centennial Photo Services, 1988).

HAND-COLORED DAGUERREOTYPES

Do you own any cased images that are hand colored? The history of photography is full of examples of hand-colored images from the early daguerreotype period to the digitally colored images of today.

Powders, paints, crayons, and pastels were all used to make photographs look more lifelike. These tinted enhancements range from delicately shaded pink lips and gold jewelry to elaborate coloring that obscures the image and transforms a photograph into a painting.

Some photographers hired artists to apply the color, while others attempted to do the job themselves. The final results were mixed based on the skill of the person laying down the color.

In his 1852 book, *A System of Natural Philosophy*, John Comstock provides details about how tints might've been added to daguerreotypes along with a bit of background on coloring in general:

Coloring daguerreotype pictures is an American invention, and has been considered a secret, though at the present time it is done with more or less success by most artists. The color consists of the oxyds [sic] of several metals, ground to an impalpable powder. They are laid on in a dry state, with soft camel-hair pencils, after the process of gilding. The plate is then heated by which they are fixed. This is a very delicate part of the art, and should not be undertaken by those who have not a good eye, and a light hand.

Comstock received these details from a Mr. N.G. Burgess of 192 Broadway, New York, and claimed that "he was an experienced and expert artist in this line." According to information on Craig's Daguerreian Registry **<www.craigcamera.com/dag>** Nathan Burgess appears to be one of the earliest daguerreotypists in this country.

The photo in this sidebar, taken c.1855 by Tyler & Co., is an example of a hand-colored daguerreotype. The photographer tinted the men's jackets a gray color, but the red details are what stand out the most. Additional information on Tyler can be found in Craig's Daguerreian Registry.

Note: If you were looking at the original of this image, you'd have to view the image at an angle. This is a key characteristic of a daguerreotype. They were often also reversed.

The foremen from the Phoenix Fire Company and Mechanic Fire Company of Charleston, South Carolina.

Sometimes identifying an image involves more than just putting a name with a face; it includes dating the enclosure—frame, mat, or case—in which it was found. Understanding these cased gems is a snap when you ask a series of questions and consult useful resources. Let's use the cased image Carole Dolisi Bean discovered in her great-grandmother Elizabeth Moll Dolisi's sewing box to illustrate the identification process for these types of pictures.

What type of photograph is it?

Identifying the type of photograph helps determine when the image was taken.

Daguerreotypes: 1839–c.1860

Ambrotypes: 1854–c.1865

Tintypes: 1856–twentieth century

Paper prints: 1840–present

All of these can be found in cases. If you have to hold the image at an angle to view it, then it's a daguerreotype. Ambrotype emulsion tends to flake off the back of the glass, so if you can see through the picture, it is an ambrotype. Use clothing clues to establish a time frame when unable to identify the photographic method. Resist the temptation to remove the image from its case — doing so can cause irreparable damage to both the picture and the case. In this instance, the image is a paper print, easily identifiable because the cover glass is missing.

How was the case made?

Cases are a compilation of materials—the case itself, liner, photograph, mat, glass, and preserver. Different styles of clasps and hinges held all the parts together, such as the hook and eye used on this example.

Cases came in a variety of sizes, shapes, and formats from simple to elaborate, so the composition and design of the exterior can establish a date for it. Bean's wooden framed case is not an unusual format or size, and the exterior geometric design was fairly common. Wood framed cases were popular in the 1840s and 1850s before being replaced by "union cases," which were constructed from a variety of substances. It is safe to theorize that this case was assembled in the 1840s or 1850s.

Liners of various shades of velvet cushioned the inside of most cases. Adorned with patterns, some even bear the name of the manufacturer. The simple scroll pattern in the Bean case doesn't include any maker's information.

Brass mats frame the cased image, while the thin brass preservers seal the photograph, mat, and glass into the case to keep them from falling out and to protect the image from the elements. Mats and preservers from the 1840s are plain, but by the 1850s they sported embossed designs. Since the mat in this example is fairly elaborate, we can hypothesize that it was created in the 1850s.

All the evidence in the case owned by Bean—wood frame and ornate mat—identify it as being assembled in the 1850s. Does the photographic evidence agree with the case? Let's see.

Clothing Clues

The man is wearing a loose sack coat with a velvet collar, patterned vest, white shirt, and a colorful tie. Starting in 1854, men's jackets were a looser fit than earlier in the decade—so it is likely this picture was taken later than the mid-1850s. Based on his clothing, this portrait was taken in circa 1860. Compare the clothing worn in your photographs against images in Joan L. Severa's *Dressed for the Photographer: Ordinary Americans and Fashion, 1840–1900* (Kent, Ohio: Kent State University Press, 1995).

CAROLE DOLISI BEAN

Interpreting the Evidence

After the popularity of cased photographs waned in the late nineteenth century, individuals discarded the images and used the cases for other pictures. As a result, many daguerreotypes, ambrotypes, tintypes, and even paper prints that originally sat in cases now lie unprotected in family collections. Part of evaluating the evidence is determining whether the picture is original to the case. In this example, the date of this case and the photograph (circa 1860) are the same, which suggests that the photographer placed the portrait in this case.

Carole Bean hoped that the young man in his twenties was her great-grandmother's brother, August Edward Moll, born 1857. The clues don't match this identification, however. August would not be the right age for this picture. Whoever this is, he must have been a special person for Elizabeth Moll Dolisi to store his picture in her sewing box for safe-keeping and to gaze upon when stitching.

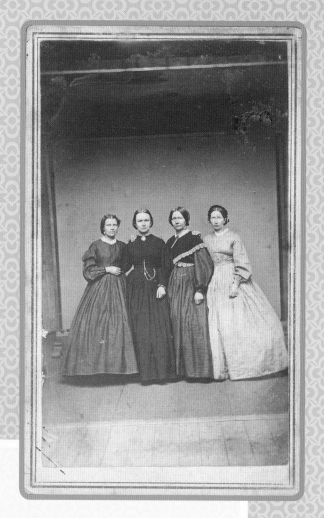

"Card portraits, as everyone knows, have-become the social currency, the 'green-backs' of civilization."

—Oliver Wendell Holmes, 1863

4

Paper Prints and Negatives

By the 1850s, our ancestors could select the method of photography that they wanted for their portrait. The daguerreotype, ambrotype, tintype, and card photograph were all available. Some of these processes were on the decline, while others were just coming to the public's notice. Studios advertised the types of images they could produce to attract customers. In the competitive early photography market, photographers needed to be equally proficient in all the techniques in order to survive.

1840
Sir John Herschel first uses the term "positive image" for photographs.

1850
Frederick Scott Archer discovers a method of using light-sensitive collodion to create the first wet-plate glass negative.

1860
A tintype is used as a campaign button for the first time.

1861
The first patent is issued for a photograph album.

1864
Marcus A. Root publishes *The Camera and the Pencil*, the first history of American photography.

By the end of the 1860s, card photographs became the pre-eminent medium for portraits, and daguerreotypes and ambrotypes began to disappear in favor of the print. Paper prints developed at the same time as the daguerreotype, but did not achieve popularity until the process of making multiple prints was introduced. Like many of the early processes, the paper print was invented in Europe and later came to the United States.

Inexpensive to produce, durable, and available in quantity, the paper image remains a common photographic process despite the popularity of digital images.

TALBOTYPES: THE FIRST PAPER PRINTS

The first paper print was the talbotype. While Louis Daguerre was developing the daguerreotype, an Englishman named William Henry Fox Talbot found a way to produce pictures on paper. These talbotypes never enjoyed the popularity of the daguerreotype in the United States. Talbot ensured his own failure when he required strict patent enforcement.

Talbotypes can be easily identified. The print was produced from a waxed paper negative, so the images lack sharpness and clarity.

Other early paper photographs based on Talbot's discovery were common in England, France, and possibly Canada from about 1840–1860. These prints are composed of rag-based paper (such as quality writing paper), sodium chloride (table salt), and silver nitrate (a light sensitive chemical). Photos produced using paper negatives were called calotypes, but those produced with a glass negative were referred to by the general term salted paper print. James M. Reilly's *The Albumen Salted Paper Book: The History and Practice of Photographic Printing, 1840–1895* (Rochester, NY: Light Impressions, 1980), available online at <**http://albumen. conservation-us.org/library/monographs/reilly/**>, explains how these images were created. Both produced sharper images than the talbotype process.

CARD PHOTOGRAPHS

The most popular type of paper print was the card photograph, which was essentially a paper print mounted on cardboard stock. *Cartes de visite*, cabinet cards, and stereographs are three types of card photographs. The size of the card varied from *cartes de visite* which were 2 ½" × 4¼" to the Imperial or life-size cabinet cards, which were 6⅞" × 9⅞". There were at least twenty different types of cards. The majority of cards in your collection are probably *cartes de visite* or cabinet cards. By the 1880s, cabinet cards replaced the smaller cards in popularity.

It's unclear who invented the small card photographs known as *cartes de visite*, but they became popular in 1854 when Frenchman Andre Adolphe Eugene Disderi developed a camera that could take eight pictures in one negative. The resulting prints, mounted to calling-card sized cardboard, could be left with friends during visits. They began appearing in the United States in 1859.

Collecting cards of royalty and other famous individuals became a pastime encouraged by the mass production of photographs of newsworthy events and famous people. Booksellers, publishers, and photographers sold them to augment their income. They could sell thousands of copies of a popular image. There may

Early paper prints were known as cartes de visites or visiting cards, 1860s.

Card Photographs	Sizes	Year Introduced
Boudoir	5¼" × 8½"	not known
Cabinet card	4½" × 6½"	1866
Cartes de visite	4¼" × 2½"	process introduced in U.S. 1859
Imperial (life-size)	6⅞" × 9⅞"	not known
Panel	8¼" × 4"	not known
Promenade	4" × 7"	1875
Stereograph	either 3" × 7" or 4" × 7"	1859 1870
Victoria	3¼" × 5"	1870

be an album of nineteenth-century card photographs in your family's photograph collection that is not of family members, but of the royalty or celebrities of the time.

Cartes de visite were primarily albumen prints. These prints consist of paper stock of various thicknesses coated with egg whites. A photograph was taken by exposing a glass negative coated with collodion to light while in the camera. The negative would then be placed against the coated paper and left in sunlight. The exposure to the sun developed the picture. Washing the print in chemical baths and toning it with gold chloride gave albumen prints a brownish color. These early prints tended to fade.

It is possible to establish an approximate date for a card photograph based on its size. A more exact date can only be determined based on other information contained in the image.

There are so many different types of prints that telling them apart is difficult. Nineteenth-century paper prints are a rainbow of colors, from the brilliant blue of cyanotypes to the soothing gray of platinum prints. The color may also depend on the toning that has been used to tint the image. It is difficult to identify the photographic process used for a card photograph unless you are trained in photo identification using a microscope.

STEREOGRAPHS

A stereoscopic image is composed of two nearly identical images mounted side-by-side. A special camera with two lenses mounted two and one-half inches apart took

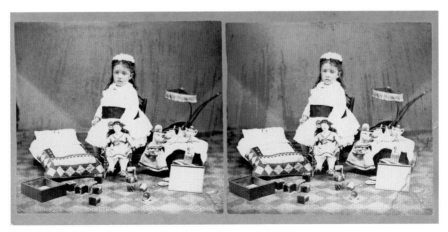

COLLECTION OF THE AUTHOR

Stereographs allowed viewers to see scenes in 3D, c.1870s.

TYPES OF STEREOGRAPHS	
Daguerreotypes	1850–1854
Glass	1854–1862
Porcelain	1854–1858
Card	1854–1938

RESOURCES FOR STEREOGRAPHS

Iowa Stereographs: Three-Dimensional Visions of the Past by Mary Bennett and Paul C. Juhl (Iowa City: University of Iowa Press, 1997).

Stereo Views: An Illustrated History & Price Guide by John Waldsmith, 2d ed. (Iola, WS: Krause Publications, 2002).

Stereoviews: A History of Stereographs in America and Their Collection by William C. Darrah (Gettysburg, PA: Times and News Publishing Co., 1964).

The World of Stereographs by William C. Darrah (Nashville, TN.: Land Yacht Press, 1998).

the picture. The distance between the lenses matches the average distance between two eyes. This calculation allows the image to appear three-dimensional when examined through a special viewer.

Stereoscopic images could be created in any photographic medium, but they are primarily paper prints mounted on a cardboard stock. The purpose of the stereograph was to provide entertainment. A few companies produced sets of images on millions of different subjects, including travel, wartime scenes, transportation, and religious subjects. The reverse side of the card contained a label with information on the photographer or publisher and the title and subject. This is very helpful when trying to date the image.

CANDID PHOTOGRAPHY

In the 1880s, a new type of paper print appeared. While studios had produced all the card photographs, they were about to have competition from an unlikely source—amateurs. The age of candid photography began with the slogan, "You push the button, we do the rest." George

COLLECTION OF THE AUTHOR

Candid photography allowed individuals to take pictures of their everyday life, c.1914.

Some of those unidentified photographs in your collection or albums may not depict your family. Long before People magazine, our ancestors were fascinated by the famous and infamous of their generation, and they collected photographs of them. Sold by bookstores, stationery shops, and individual photographers, these images often ended up in family albums.

These aren't the only images our ancestors collected. They purchased photographs of local landmarks, Civil War heroes, royalty, and theatrical personalities. People of all ages collected images that appealed to their individual interests, added them to photo albums, and showed them off to company. My children do much the same thing with trading cards today. Even if these images don't depict family members, you can still learn something about your ancestors by studying them. Start by asking yourself the following questions as you analyze your mystery photos.

TERRI MAHAR

Is it a family portrait?

Terri Mahar found this portrait, with the photographer's imprint, "Geo. H. McDonald, 289 W. Madison St., Chicago," in a group of unidentified family photographs that she inherited from a relative. While she has a McDonald line, she's not sure if she's related to the photographer of this scene. This might be a photograph bought merely for entertainment, not to commemorate family. Handwritten on the image is "Rca Baby" and "McDonald & Towser." It appears that the photographer posed with his dog Towser. Why? Who knows. Pet owners have posed with their animals since the beginning of photography. In trying to imitate the look on his dog's face, McDonald created a picture funny enough to be sold through a distributor. It was probably printed in a limited quantity.

How did it get there?

The question isn't who is in the picture, but how it became part of Mahar's family photo collection. It's possible that someone in her family purchased the picture in Chicago, or that a friend sent it to a relative as a joke. Perhaps the family owned a similar breed of dog. Mahar should look for proof of a trip to Chicago, a note from the sender, or a picture of the family with their pet.

Who owned it?

According to William C. Darrah's *Cartes de Visite in Nineteenth Century Photography* (Gettysburg, Pa.: W.C. Darrah, 1981), chocolate-colored card stock was popular between 1877 and 1887. This ten-year time frame narrows down the possible owners to those living in that time period.

Whom does it depict?

The caption tells us who is in this picture. To find out if McDonald and his dog were famous, or if similar images exist, I typed their names into different Internet search engines such as Google **<www.google.com>** and Yahoo **<www.yahoo.com>** (any will do, just remember to try more than one—you never know which one might ferret out the tidbit you're looking for). Unfortunately, nothing turned up.

If an image remains a mystery, there are books that can help you find more clues. Darrah's book has a wide variety of photographs to use for comparison, and *The Photographic Experience, 1839–1914: Images and Attitudes* by Heinz K. and Bridget A. Henisch (University Park: Pennsylvania State University Press, 1994) explores the history of photography and how it was used.

Eastman developed an easy to use roll film camera that anyone could operate. He called it the Kodak.

Amateur photographers could take as many as one hundred pictures per roll with the first models. After taking a picture, the photographer turned a key to advance the film to a new exposure. When all the pictures on a roll were taken, the photographer sent the camera back to the manufacturer to process the film, make a set of prints, and reload the camera with new film. Later improvements allowed photographers to load the film themselves and send it for development without the camera.

Kodak marketed its cameras to women and children; no longer were men the only photographers in the family. The Kodak Brownie camera inspired generations of both ordinary and famous children to follow their dream of photography, allowing them to take candid photographs of their everyday lives. The Brownie was a mass marketing marvel—almost a quarter million were sold in the year it was introduced. Kodak reached out to the untapped youth market in the United States and abroad with a camera "any school age boy or girl could easily operate." The Brownie was especially suitable for children because of its simplicity, size, and good snapshot result. It sold for a dollar, well within the means of any frugal child. The Brownie became a cultural icon, embraced by millions regardless of age or gender and used for generations. The cultural ramifications of this simple low-cost invention are still felt today in the market for disposable cameras, which are used by children and adults as well as amateur and professional photographers.

Kodak used the sprightly "Brownie" figure created by Canadian illustrator Palmer Cox as a marketing tool. Youngsters, personified by the Brownie Boy in advertisements, grabbed the opportunity to photograph their world. Twelve-year-old Ansel Adams, given a Brownie by his parents as a birthday present, used it to take his first pictures of Half Dome in Yosemite. Kodak representatives taught the children of Tsar Nicholas II of Russia how to use their camera. Seventeen-year-old Bernice Palmer, a passenger on the *Carpathia*, captured the sinking of the Titanic with her Brownie. Child stars of the 1930s and 1940s, such as Jane Withers, took their Brownies to the set to candidly photograph their famous co-stars. Average children around the world filled scrapbooks full of family portraits and activities.

With the Brownie, children found a new creative outlet. They selected their subjects and props and arranged their own photographic albums. There were publications, clubs, and contests all directed at the youth

CHARACTERISTICS OF DIFFERENT PRINTS

Type of Photograph	Date Introduced	Characteristics
Albumen print	1855	Fades; tiny cracks in the image; colors same as salted paper print; paper fibers visible
Carbon print	1860	No fading; large cracks in dark areas
Cyanotype	1880	Blue
Gelatin developing out	1885	No paper fibers; reflective dark areas resemble a silver color
Gelatin printing out paper or collodion	1885	Purple image; no paper fibers visible
Matte collodion	1894	No fading; some paper fibers visible
Platinotype	1880	No fading
Salted paper print	1840	Yellow-brown or red-brown; fades
Woodburytype	1866	No fading; some cracking in dark areas

market. Fictional children's stories and popular series, such as Tom Swift, featured camera-toting children. The Brownie remained in production for eighty years.

The wide availability of these cameras made for amateurs helped create the majority of photographs in our family collections. The cameras were inexpensive and easy to use. Our ancestors found themselves free to pose and clown in front of the camera, recording memorable events and playful activities.

The size of the images varied according to the type of box camera used. The film and the cameras remained in use in families for generations. Kodak roll-film 101, introduced in 1895, had a picture area of 3½" x 3½" and wasn't discontinued until 1956. While you might be able to establish the earliest date for a photograph based on its size, it is the information in the image that will likely provide a more specific date.

DATING PAPER PRINTS

Paper prints can be dated by identifying the photographic process and by noting the thickness of the paper on which it is mounted. One expert on card photographs

COLLECTION OF THE AUTHOR

Throughout the nineteenth century, paper prints came in a variety of sizes, shapes, and colors.

CARD STOCK COLORS AND SHAPES		
Dates	Colors	Shape
1858–1869	White, gray or tan (1861–1866)	Square corners
1869–1871	Yellow, white	Square corners
1869–1875	Light orange, white, tan and light yellow	Round Corners (1871–1881)
1873–1880	Deep read, green, blue, lavender, white	Rounded corners
1877–1887	Chocolate brown/black	Rounded corners
1883–1888	White, colored cards often a different color either gray or pink on the reverse	Beveled edges common
1889–1892	White dominates	Serrated edges, beveled
1893–1896	White card stock	Variety of shapes

suggests that dating card stock using identifiers, such as shape of corners and type of image, is highly accurate plus or minus a couple of years.

Determining Card Thickness

You could invest in calipers to measure thickness or you can use an ordinary sheet of bond paper. Standard 20 lb. paper is 0.004 inch (.1 mm) thick. In general, card stock is as follows for cartes de visite:

1858–1869= six or less sheets of bond

1869–1887= seven or eight sheets

Thank you to Andrew Morris of Dating 19th Century Photographs <**www.familychronicle.com/ Dating19thCenturyPhotos.html**> for this succinct description.

There are other indicators that are more reliable than card thickness, such as color and style of the card. See the Card Stock Colors and Shapes sidebar for a list of these indicators.

DATING PORTRAITS

Did you know that the placement of sitters in the portrait can reveal relationships within your family? Examine the portrait to determine who is the predominant individual. The dominant member of the family is usually the central figure. Traditionally, this is either the father or mother, but not always. The main figure can also be the individual who arranged for the portrait or the most successful member of the family. Young children and babies sit on the laps of the people in the front row. When looking at portraits in your collection, consider the following questions: Who is standing in the back? Are the children arranged in birth order? Is there anyone absent from the photograph? Be careful not to overlook details that could prove valuable later. The answers to these questions can lead you to an identification. For example, in a family portrait, you may know the name of one person but not the rest. If the children are posed

RESOURCES FOR CARD PHOTOGRAPHS

Care and Identification of 19th Century Photographic Prints by James M. Reilly (Rochester, N.Y.: Eastman Kodak Publications, 1986).

Cartes de Visite in Nineteenth Century Photography by William Darrah (Gettysburg, PA: W.C. Darrah, 1981).

Victorian Costume for Ladies 1860-1900 by Linda Setnik (Atglen,PA: Schiffer, 2000).

in birth order, you might be able to identify them based on information from your family group sheets.

Identifying the people in a portrait often depends on when the picture was taken. The style of a portrait can help you date the image—different poses were popular at different times. Vignettes from 1860–1870 were headshots, which literally just showed the head and sometimes the shoulders of the subject. During other time periods, it was more common to have a portrait showing the whole subject. Clues for dating this type of portrait would include the size, the amount of the figure that is shown, and whether the person appears seated or standing.

Decorative elements in portraits are another way to date an image. They ranged from an embossed frame around the image to a plain window. Photographers could also place the picture within an ornamental background or cut it into a decorative shape. Patrons could choose from a wide variety of patterns and designs. A good guide to posing and card design appears in Darrah's book *Cartes de Visite in Nineteenth Century Photography*.

DATING THE CARD STOCK OF STEREOGRAPHS

Card stock can be identified by color, shape of the corners, and type of image. (The data in these charts is based on information presented in William Darrah's *Stereoviews: A History of Stereographs in America and Their Collection*.

OTHER DATING CLUES

The next time you take out your unidentified photographs for another wistful look, instead of focusing on the front, turn to the back. The back of the image may be more interesting and informative than the picture itself. You may find something there that can help you narrow down possible identifications or establish a date. Here are a few things to look for.

Revenue Stamps

On 1 August 1864, the United States government levied a tax on photographs. For two years, until 1 August 1866, photographers had to affix a stamp to the back of their images. In addition, they were required to hand cancel each stamp with their name or initials and the date of

STEREOTYPE CHARACTERISTICS BY YEAR

Square Corners Color	Date
White, cream, or gray lustrous	1854–1862
Dull gray	1860–1863
Canary yellow or chrome yellow	1862–1868
Blue, green, red, yellow	1865–1870

Rounded Corners Type	Date
Photographs	1868–1882
Copied photographs	1873–1878
Printed	1874–1878

Card Mounts, Curved Color	Date
Buff mounts, thick card	1879–1906
Gray mounts	1893–1940
Black mounts	1902–1908

TAX STAMP RATES

Tax	Photo Selling Price
2¢	less than 25¢
3¢	25¢ to 50¢
5¢	50¢ to $1
5¢	for each additional $1

Tax stamps could be combined for added value. A modification to the law in March 1865 lowered the tax on images that cost less than 10 cents to 1 cent each. Stamps included information on their original usage such as the "playing card" stamp used in mid-1866.

Examples of Revenue Stamps

sale. The handwritten date is the exact day the photograph was sold. That date can help you compile a list of ancestors living in the right place and time—match the sex and age, and you might have an identification.

The stamp also supplies you with a little bit of social history to add to your genealogy. The value of the stamps tells you how much the picture cost. For more on this topic, see Kathleen Fuller's "Civil War Stamp Duty: Photography as a Revenue Source," in *History of Photography* 4 (October 1980): 263–282.

Captions

Captions can help or hinder you in your efforts to identify a photograph. Partial data such as a first name or a relationship ("Sister of Louise") will definitely increase your odds of putting a name with a face. However, in some cases captions are just plain misleading. Many individuals with good intentions write names on the back of images without verifying what is plausible. They might have the right name but the wrong date, or they could have several individuals with the same name on the family tree. Sometimes only a tentative relationship is known. Until you can assess all the clues in a picture, be cautious about accepting caption data. Don't jump to a conclusion that cannot be supported by facts

Picture Number

Pay attention to any numbers on the back of an image. It's not likely you'll find a collection of a photographer's negatives all numbered and waiting for you to request a copy, but since families tended to visit the same photographer for all their portraits, you might be able to establish a relationship based on picture numbers. If you have a portrait of a young woman with the number 105 on the back, look at all your photographs in a similar format by the same photographer. If you find portraits numbered 104 and 106, you may have found the woman's siblings or parents.

The backs of your photographs add to the story of your family just as much as the pictures on the front do, if you know what to look for. Remember the golden rule of dating photographs: Photo identification is the sum total of all the clues. You'll need to examine the front and the back of the picture for evidence to reach a logical conclusion.

NEGATIVES

Prior to collodion negatives in the 1860s, the number of lenses on a camera limited the quantity of prints that could be produced. With the discovery of the negative process, there was no longer any limit. Since all prints in the nineteenth century were actually contact prints, the dimension of the negative determined the size of the picture. A contact print is produced when a negative is placed on a surface treated with light-sensitive chemicals.

Negatives consist of a support surface—usually glass or film—and a coating of a light-sensitive material, such as collodion, gelatin, nitrocellulose, or cellulose acetate. The vast majority of nineteenth-century negatives were glass. Glass negatives were either wet plate or dry plate. Wet-plate negatives had to be damp when used. Photographers made them immediately prior to use by coating glass with collodion. The dry-plate process revolutionized photography, because now photographers could buy materials ready-to-use instead of having to prepare the surface themselves. The amount of equipment necessary to take photographs was substantially reduced.

CHARACTERISTICS OF GLASS NEGATIVES		
Collodion, also known as wet plate	Thick glass; edges ground; gray coating; produced by individual photographer	1851–c.1880
Gelatin, dry plate	Thin glass; uniform thickness; edges sharp; black coating; factory produced	c.1880–1920

CHARACTERISTICS OF FILM NEGATIVES		
Eastman American film—gelatin	Brittle; edges uneven	1884–c.1890
Roll film—clear plastic	Nitrocellulose; thin; curls and wrinkles easily	1889–1903
Roll film—clear plastic	Coated on both sides with gelatin to prevent curling	1903–1939
Sheet film—clear plastic	Machine-cut sheet; rectangular; edges stamped with "Eastman"	1913–1939
Roll film—clear plastic	Cellulose acetate; marked with "safety" on the edge	1939–present

The film negatives that we use today began with the Kodak process of the 1880s. The support surface was a type of clear plastic, and the negative material varied.

Home photograph collections may or may not contain negatives. If you have film negatives in your family materials, examine them carefully.

Help for Identifying Negatives

Identifying the type of negatives in your collection and the time period in which they were used is easier than identifying nineteenth-century prints. The chart on page 55 is a guide to negatives based on their characteristics. Bear in mind that photographers often used up supplies they had on-hand before moving on to a new medium. The end dates of usage may not be firm.

OTHER PHOTOGRAPHIC FORMATS

You may find photographs in places other than the traditional case or photo album. Any substance that could be coated with a light-sensitive chemical or serve as a case for early photographic formats could contain a picture. In my family, we have a pillowcase with my grandmother's picture on it. I'm not sure why she selected this format; we never asked and she never told. Photographs on fabric, leather, glass, or metal are not that unusual. Jewelry that incorporated a photograph became a popular way to remember a loved one.

Photographic Jewelry

The history of photographic jewelry spans from the daguerreotype to the present. Jewelry that contains an image combines decoration (jewelry) with function (reminder of a loved one). The photographic method dictated the style of jewelry. Daguerreotypes required a glass covering and appeared in traditional jewelry, such as rings, pendants, lockets, and bracelets. Tintypes took a decorative form, such as suspender clasps and belt buckles.

Worn by men, women, and children, photographic jewelry lent itself to a variety of settings depending on sex and age. Women generally selected pins, lockets, rings, and bracelets, including matched sets, and even coat buttons. Men favored keywinds (used to wind watches), watch fobs, rings, cuff links, stickpins, and coat buttons.

Before the late nineteenth century, all these pieces were custom-made for specific clients with unique images. Individuals interested in owning one could purchase it directly from a photography studio or have a jeweler insert the picture into a setting. It took skill to create the item so that the image was not damaged when set into the piece. Jewelers created specially made pieces using precious metals and marketed them to affluent clients. Costume jewelry settings made of brass also existed. With the advent of mail-order catalogs in the late nineteenth century, customers could choose photo garter buckles, belt buckles, charms, and buttons to show off paper prints or tintypes, usually covered with a piece of protective glass. Abraham Lincoln used a tintype portrait button for political campaigning.

Queen Victoria popularized photographic jewelry as a symbol of mourning when she wore pieces adorned with Prince Albert's image after his death in 1861. Most mourning pieces of photographic jewelry contain a reminder of the deceased. From 1861 to 1880, photographs appeared in lockets and brooches with a swiveling compartment to hold swatches of hair or clothing. Photographer William Bambridge of Windsor created some of the first pieces worn by Queen Victoria. She also ordered a set of nine gold lockets from Garrard & Company, possibly for her children. The jeweler Dancer designed a mourning ring for Queen Victoria that contained a photograph of Prince Albert attributed to John Jabez Edwin Mayall. The Queen wore jewelry with Albert's image for the rest of her life.

Most images included in jewelry are portraits. Usually, individuals featured in jewelry are related to the owner of the piece. You can identify the image using several factors: the type of photographic image, the clothing worn for the portrait, and the jewelry setting. The photographic method establishes a creation date for the piece, but not necessarily a time frame for the image. Since different settings faded in and out of fashion, the style and type of jewelry determines when the piece was fashionable, but not necessarily when the photo was taken. You must be careful when establishing a date for a piece of photographic jewelry—new images could be set into older pieces of jewelry, or vice versa. Costume details can be used to assign a narrower span of dates for the image. Any locks of hair, handwriting samples, fabric swatches, or other types of insertions behind the picture can help identify the subject of the piece. Examine the jewelry and the image thoroughly before deciding on a time frame.

RESOURCES FOR PHOTOGRAPHIC JEWELRY

Antique Photographic Jewelry: Tokens of Affection and Regard by Larry West and Patricia A Abbott (New York: West Companies, Inc, 2005).

Crown and Camera: The Royal Family and Photography, 1842-1910 by Frances Diamond and Roger Taylor (London: Penguin Books, 1987).

"Daguerreian Jewelry: Popular in Its Day" by Larry West and Patricia Abbott in *The Daguerreian Annual* (1990), 136-140.

Jewelry 1789–1910: The International Era by Shirley Bury (Woodbridge, Suffolk, U.K.: Antique Collectors' Club, 1991).

Jewelry in America: 1600–1900 by Martha Gandy Fales (Woodbridge, Suffolk, U.K.: Antique Collectors' Club, 1995).

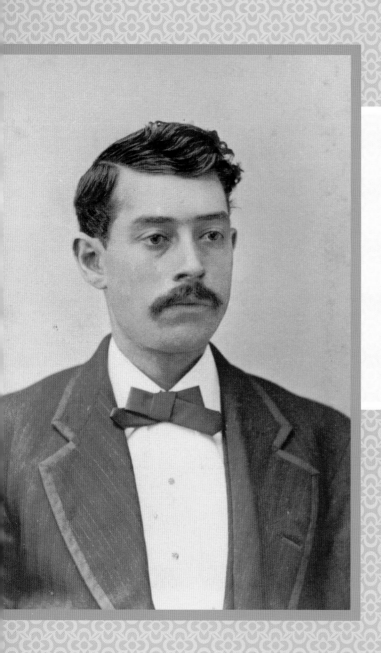

"The fact is, none of us sufficiently appreciate the nobleness and sacredness of colour."

—Oliver Wendell Holmes, 1863

5

Color and Digital Photographs

Your family photograph collection will probably contain a variety of colored images. Some will be hand-colored. In some cases the image will have just the details enhanced, such as jewelry or collars, while in others, the entire original photograph has been overpainted. One popular form of nineteenth-century portraits appears at first glance to be a charcoal drawing; however, upon close inspection, you can see the charcoal is actually just outlining the photograph.

1840s
Daguerreotypists begin coloring images using artist's materials.

1904
Augusta and Louis Lumiere patent Autochrome, the first additive color screen film material.

1963
The Polaroid Corporation, led by Dr. Edwin Land, invents the first instant color picture.

1856
Levi Hill publishes *A Treatise on Heliochromy*, which suggests that objects could be photographed in natural colors.

1935
Eastman Kodak debutes the color film Kodachrome for home movies; the next year it's introduced in a 35mm format.

Clues in hand-colored images or color prints can help you both date your collection and learn something intimate about the ancestor pictured. While the coloring technique itself usually can't date a hand-colored image (but can show you the color of someone's eyes), a color photograph can be dated by the technique by which it was produced.

Although we take color for granted as a medium for family photographs, it was virtually unavailable until Kodak introduced amateur color photography in 1936. Instead, photographers had to use a variety of techniques to add color to images. Many studios employed colorists to highlight details or enhance images.

HAND-COLORING

As early as 1841, photographers were seeking methods to add color to their images. As much as the popular press discussed the virtues of the daguerreotype, they criticized the absence of color. Photographers sought ways to increase the realism of their images. Since production of a color image was not yet possible, they improvised. Artistic mediums such as colored powders, oil paints, crayons, and charcoal were used to bring rosy cheeks and blue eyes to their subjects.

Hand-coloring accomplished several things. Early photographers wanted to impress their customers with high-quality images, and color was a way to satisfy them.

Adding color created contrast and improved upon any imperfections in the image. Since early paper prints had a tendency to fade, colorists used charcoal to trace the image. Overpainting with a variety of substances was also used to reduce fading.

Colorists, usually artists, would add color to photographs to emphasize certain details. In some cases, so much color was added, it is difficult to determine whether the pictures are paintings or photographs. In reality, they are hybrids, combining elements of both media. You may have images in your collection that appear to be paintings but are actually hand-colored images.

There were many different methods used to color photographs. Manuals contained specific instructions on what features to color. Facial features could be improved by emphasizing the cheeks, nostrils, brow, chin, and bridge of the nose. Other commonly colored parts of a photograph were the hands, draperies, clothing, and background of the image.

The palette of colors depended on what was being colored. For example, jewelry and buttons were enhanced with gold, while pink was added to cheeks. Skilled technicians would add color to clothing. Everything from white collars to plaid garments could be improved with a little color. In one family's collection, a black-and-white photograph contains the photographer's hand-

JANE SCHWERDTFEGER

All types of images could be hand-colored, including these arcade portraits, c.1910.

Could this be the wedding picture of Elizabeth Goza and William Harrington, who married in 1846? The image passed from Geri Diehl's grandmother to her mother and ultimately came to be in her collection. The picture is a crayon portrait, in which the photographer or an artist colored the couple's eyes and parts of the background blue.

It is most likely a copy photograph of an earlier image. Since it is a copy, we can't be absolutely certain of a time frame without being able to compare it to the original. In an artistically enhanced portrait, costume elements were sometimes altered to be more current than the original. The woman's clothing lacks detail that could help assign a definite date—however, several costume features suggest a date from the late 1850s, which would rule it out as the Goza/Harrington wedding photo.

The man is wearing a double-breasted, shawl-collared vest of a style from the 1850s. His jacket has darker trim on the upper lapel and collar, which is not usual for either 1846 or the 1850s. One of the determining factors is his collar. In the 1840s, most men wore their collars standing up. His being in a different style would suggest the photo was not taken in the 1840s. Also, the man's hair is blunt cut and he has a mustache and goatee, characteristics found in photographs from the 1850s.

It is unfortunate that the artist chose to represent the woman's dress as solid black without sleeve and bodice details—the shape of the sleeves and bodice can be used to date an image. The artist spent time enhancing her collar and gold-tinting her broach and earrings. The style of her small drop earrings also confirms that the portrait was not taken in 1846, but in the 1850s. The woman is

Geri Diehl and Alan Spiven

wearing her hair with a center part and a low bun behind her ears. In the 1840s women generally wore their hair looped over their ears. In the late 1850s and early 1860s, women wore their hair in the style shown in this portrait. Her wide collar of whitework became fashionable in the 1850s and is the primary evidence that the portrait was not taken in 1846. Dress collars were a different shape and style in the 1840s.

Family members suspect that this was a wedding portrait of the Goza/ Harrington couple, but the photographic evidence doesn't agree with the marriage date. It could be a portrait the couple had taken later in their marriage or a different couple.

coloring instructions: "dark grey (sic) eyes, light golden hair, golden brown velvet suit, pearl buttons, cream collar and cuffs, and green peach leaves in hand."

Different photographic methods required different types of coloring techniques. A daguerreotype's metal surface could be enhanced with colored powders. They could be applied by using a brush or by gently blowing the colors onto the surface. Paper prints were easier to color than daguerreotypes since paper is a traditional painting surface. The tools used were the same as those for painting portraits: brushes and colors. In a few examples, photographic artists added individuals to the original photograph.

In addition to hand-coloring, photographers added details through retouching. The wavy hair in this portrait was enhanced with pencil.

RETOUCHING

The need for the enhancements increased with the introduction of larger prints. A slight flaw that was barely visible in a carte de visite portrait was a major imperfection in the larger card photographs.

Photographers generally used retouching to eliminate bothersome flaws in negatives—it was more economical to fix the negative before prints were made. Tiny flaws in the negative could be filled in with pencil or charcoal. Retouching could eliminate minor blemishes, stray hairs, and distractions, while major changes to the negative could be made by actually scraping away some of the emulsion. In this way, significant changes to the original image could be introduced without damaging the photograph.

COLOR PHOTOGRAPHY

There were several attempts to produce color images in the nineteenth century, but none were particularly successful or easy to duplicate. It wasn't until 1904 that the first commercially successful color photography process was introduced. Developed by Auguste and Louis Lumiere, it was called the Autochrome. This process used starch grains dyed red, green, and blue to create a positive image. A photographer could insert the plate in the camera, expose it to light, and develop it. A special viewer called a "diascope" was needed to view the transparency. Photographs of scenes and individuals could be taken, but this process was used by professional photographers and rarely appears in family collections.

For another three decades, color photography remained a commercial venture in the hands of professional photographers and printers. It wasn't until 1935 that the first color film for amateurs became available—Kodak's Kodachrome 16mm motion picture film. The retail price of a roll of the film when it was first introduced was $7.75 for one hundred feet. In 1936, Kodachrome became available in an 8mm format and as slides.

Negative film became available from Kodak in 1941. Just as the early daguerreotypists advised individuals to wear certain colors to obtain a good likeness, so did Kodak. The company printed a manual to guide family photographers that contained a chart of acceptable clothing colors and background choices. The intensity of Kodacolor could be distracting if bright colors were worn against a colorful background.

POLAROID

In 1947, Edwin Land patented a process for producing black-and-white pictures that developed in a minute. This was the first time amateur photographers did

BOOKS ON EARLY COLOR PHOTOS

The Art of the Autochrome: the Birth of Color Photography by John Wood (Iowa City: University of Iowa Press, 1993).

A Half Century of Color by Louis Walton Sipley (New York: Macmillan Co., 1951).

Kodachrome and How to Use It by Ivan Dimitri (New York: Simon and Schuster, 1940).

The Painted Photograph, 1839–1914: Origins, Techniques, Aspirations by Heinz K. and Bridget Henisch (University Park, PA: Pennsylvania State University Press, 1996).

not have to send their film to a lab for developing. The quality of the photograph could be judged immediately and reshot if necessary. Initially offered as a black-and-white process, Polaroid didn't have color film available to the public until 1963. Close to 65 percent of the billion Polaroid pictures taken that year were in color. Most of them were family photographs. Polaroid maintained its appeal to amateur photographers by offering new and improved cameras every few years.

Each Polaroid picture contains a line code number on the back that refers to the date of manufacture and/or the type of film.

- From 1948–1965, Polaroid manufactured many cameras that used several early roll films. Types 32 and 37 black and white film had a picture sized 2½" x 3¼"; Types 42 and 47 black and white film had a picture sized 3¼" x 4¼"; and Type 48 color film's photo size was also 3¼" x 4¼". Type 30 Series roll film was discontinued in the late 1980s and Series 40 film followed in 1992.

- Pack film began in 1963 and continues to the present. It's manufactured in color and black and white and has a picture size of 3¼" x 4¼" with an image area of 2⅞" x 3¾".

- Integral film was introduced in 1972, and on the back bottom of each photo appears a number, identifying when it was manufactured. The photo measures 3½" x 4¼" with an image area of 3⅛" squared.

- Spectra cameras were introduced in 1986 and use a different size of integral film. The photo is 4" square and the image area is 3⅝" x 2⅞". Numbers on the back of the picture indicate when the film was made.

A list of Polaroid cameras appears on Wikipedia, **<en.wikipedia.org/wiki/List_of_Polaroid_instant_cameras>** but it doesn't contain specifics on image dimensions.

DIGITAL PHOTOGRAPHS

In 1975, an engineer at Eastman Kodak used a camera with image sensor chips that weighed eight pounds and took twenty-three seconds to capture the scene. While a digital camera was used at the 1984 Summer Olympics and during the first Gulf War, the first commercially successful digital cameras didn't debut until 1990. The technology has come a long way since then. Now we

have cameras small enough to carry in a pocket. You can learn more about the history of digital cameras at **<www.digicamhistory.com>**. If you own an older digital camera, you might be able to help with this online project to identify older cameras.

Identifying Digital Images

File names can be very helpful in identifying and dating digital images. Create a file name that helps to identify the people in the image. The challenge is to keep the file name short but useful. Also include the date of creation in the file name. Some digital cameras embed information, such as date and location in the digital file.

"I got a fine likeness of my sister at Whipple's last-week..."

— Letter from Caroline Cushman to Henry Wyles Cushman (from the Cushman Collection in the New England Historic Genealogical Society)

6

Identifying the Photographer

Identifying a photographer's dates and places of operation is the most straightforward task involved in photo research. These two little pieces of information can help you place an ancestral portrait within a particular time period. When this data is pieced together with your genealogical research and other clues in the image, it may enable you to name the individual in the picture.

1840
Frenchman Francois Gouraud holds public lectures and demonstrations of the daguerreotype in Boston, Massachusetts, and Providence, Rhode Island.

1850
Mathew Brady publishes his Gallery of Illustrious Americans, which contains portraits and biographies of eminent American citizens.

1859
John P. Soule establishes the Soule Art company and sells images of notable nineteenth century personages.

1861–1865
Itinerant photographers travel with military units during the Civil War, providing soldiers with pictures for loved ones at home.

1900
A quarter of a million Kodak Brownie Camera's were sold for one dollar each.

1905–1920
Photographic postcards reach their peak popularity.

PHOTOGRAPHER'S IMPRINT

A photographer's imprint will allow you to trace the business dates for that photographer or studio. There are many different varieties of imprints, including hand-written tags, embossed labels, and rubber-stamped identifications. Photographers could order preprinted cards from a supplier or stamp or write the imprint on the card themselves.

Many of the images in your family collection will have a photographer's imprint on the stock to which the image is mounted, and it's important to know where to look for it.

Cased images can have the photographer's name scratched into the plate or glass, or their name might appear on the brass mat or embossed into the velvet interior of the case. Photographers also used symbols or business cards to identify their work.

With paper mounts, the photographer's imprint may appear stamped, embossed, or handwritten on the mat. Card photographs can have imprints on either the front or back of the card. If a card photograph lacks an imprint, it may be a copy of an original card.

The imprint does not always refer to a photographer. It can be the name of a publisher or distributor. Many businesses sold card photographs published by companies other than the original photographer. The most popular were portraits of important individuals such as royalty and newsworthy events like the Civil War.

It's more difficult to locate an imprint on prints or negatives than on cased images or cards. A photographer may have scratched his name into the emulsion on the negative, but that is an exception. Paper prints can contain an embossed imprint, but identification is usually stylistic rather than preprinted.

Generally an imprint identifies the name of the studio, publisher, or photographer. The simplest ones tell just the name of the photographer, usually an initial and a surname. More elaborate imprints can contain a list of services offered, awards received, and the photographer's logo. In cases where only a surname appears, you will probably have difficulty researching that photographer. The same is true for imprints that only list the company name without the proprietor's name. An address

VARIETY OF INFORMATION IN AN IMPRINT

- Name
- Price schedules
- Address
- Instructions for the sitter
- Partnerships
- Date of establishment
- Logos
- Names of retouchers
- Advertising
- Awards
- Patent numbers or license to use a process
- Additional occupations
- Special services
- Fraternal or religious affiliations
- Negatives on file
- National origins
- Business sold to another photographer

WHERE TO FIND IMPRINTS

Daguerreotypes, Ambrotypes, Tintypes: Name may be scratched into a plate or the emulsion, similar to an artist's identification on a painting, or on the brass mat or velvet interior side of the case.

Paper Mounts: Handwritten, embossed, or stamped on the mat.

Card Photograph: On the front or back of the card.

Paper Prints: Not usually signed.

Negatives: Scratched into the emulsion.

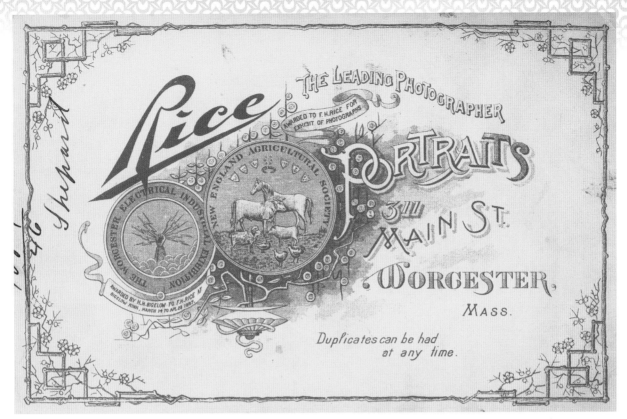

Photographer's imprints contain a wide variety of information, from awards to telephone numbers.

will enable you to place a photographer geographically and chronologically. A specific house and street number can narrow the search. An award or patent number will specify a date. Magazine articles about the award or patent will further support the information in the imprint. Each additional piece of information is another detail to be researched.

Often, an imprint will mention a partnership or the prior owner of the studio. This will assist you in trying to locate the dates of operation. Partnerships were usually short-lived and photographers, unless they had a steady clientele and solid reputation, moved around looking for better economic opportunities.

Sometimes imprints contain misspellings or a deviation in the spelling of the photographer's name. This can lead to difficulties in finding documentation. If you don't find what you are looking for the first time, try searching for similar names, such as "Smyth," if the name is spelled "Smith" in the imprint.

RESEARCHING A PHOTOGRAPHER

Once you have a name, there are several basic resources for locating photographers. Before you undertake painstaking research to locate information, try entering the name of the photographer in an online search engine, such as Google <**google.com**>. This search may lead you to a book, article, or online entry about the photo studio. Use both the general Web search engine as well as Google books <**books.google.com**>.

City or business directories, newspapers, almanacs, mug or booster books (biographical encyclopedias of important members of a community), photography magazines, and census records can all be used to locate photographers. None of these sources are complete, so consult a sampling before declaring an end to your search.

TYPES OF IMPRINTS

1. Embossed or impressed

2. Paper labels or stamps

3. Handwritten

4. Rubber-stamped name, address, and sometimes the logo of the photographer

5. Printed name and address

NATIONAL PHOTOGRAPHIC PUBLICATIONS

The Daguerreian Journal, 1850, continued as *Humphrey's Journal of Photography* until 1870

The Philadelphia Photographer, 1864–1888

The Photographic Art Journal, 1851, bought out by *American Journal of Photography* (1852) in 1861

St. Louis Photographer (later the *St. Louis and Canadian Photographer*), 1883–1910

The St. Louis Practical Photographer, 1877–1882

SOURCES

For information on photographers

- The photographer's imprint

- City directories/phone books/local histories

- Newspapers

- Census records

- Online search engines

To Find Photographers

- Directories

- Newspapers (news and obituaries)

- Mug books

- Court records

- Photography magazines

- Directories of regional photographers

- Census records, federal and state

- Special census schedules

- Online search engines

Directories appear in several formats: by locality, region, business, or house. Directories of a particular city or town appeared annually in larger cities and every few years in smaller towns. Regional or suburban listings usually included several small towns in their coverage area. Business directories contained information on the companies in the area. These are excellent sources for locating photographers. A typical listing will contain a person's name, address, occupation, and often the name of his employer. When researching photographers, this data confirms the information in the imprint.

In cases where the imprint only includes the address and a business name, you can locate the name of the owner of the studio by using a house directory. Each listing is in order by street name, followed by house or building number and the names of the occupants.

Your public library or local historical society probably has directories for your city or town. If you are researching someone outside of your local area, it may require a little more effort to find the directories you're looking for. The two largest collections of city directories are in the Library of Congress and the American Antiquarian Society in Worcester, Massachusetts. Collections of digitized directories can be found on Ancestry.com <**www.ancestry.com**> and Fold3 <**www.fold3.com**>. Start your search by using an online search engine and the keywords *city directory* plus the name of the city or town.

Directories of regional photographers, in which you may find a full description of a photographer and his works, can save you a lot of time and effort. *Photographers: A Sourcebook for Historical Research, 2d ed.*, edited by Peter Palmquist (Nevada City, Calif.: Carl Mautz Publishing, 2000) contains a worldwide bibliography of published lists of photographers by Richard Rudisill. You can also search online at Finding Photographers <**www.findingphotographers.homestead.com**>.

Chris Steele and Ron Polito's exhaustively researched *A Directory of Massachusetts Photographers, 1839–1900* (Camden, Me.: Picton Press, 1993) relied on city directories to track photographers through time. Each citation for a photographer is in three parts: business listings, residential address, and advertisements. For example, using this book to research a photograph taken by Oscar T. Higgins reveals that he operated out of several

SPECIAL CENSUS FOR INDUSTRY—1850, 1860, AND 1870

State	Location of Originals
Alabama	Alabama Department of Archives and History, Montgomery, Ala.
California	California State Library, Sacramento, Calif.
Colorado (1870 only)	Duke University Library, Durham, N.C.
Connecticut	Connecticut State Library, Hartford, Conn.
Delaware	Delaware Public Archives Commission, Dover, Del.
District of Columbia*	Duke University Library, Durham, N.C.
Florida*	Florida State University Library, Gainesville, Fla.
Idaho (1870 only)	Idaho Historical Society, Boise, Idaho
Illinois*	Illinois State Archives, Springfield, Ill.
Indiana	Indiana State Library, Indianapolis, Ind.
Iowa*	State Historical Society of Iowa Library, Des Moines, Iowa
Kansas* (1860, 1870)	Kansas State Historical Society, Topeka, Kans.
Kentucky*	Duke University Library, Durham, N.C.
Maine	Maine State Archives, Augusta, Maine
Maryland* (1850, 1860 Baltimore City, County only)	Department of Legislative Reference, City Hall, Baltimore, Md.
Massachusetts*	Commonwealth of Massachusetts State Library and Archivist of the Commonwealth, Office of the Secretary of State (duplicates), Boston, Mass.
Michigan*	State Archives of Michigan, Lansing, Mich.
Minnesota	Minnesota Historical Society, St. Paul, Minn.
Mississippi	Mississippi Department of Archives and History, Jackson, Miss.
Missouri	State Historical Society of Missouri, Columbia, Mo.
Montana* (1870)	Montana Historical Society, Helena, Mont.
Nebraska* (1860, 1870)	Nebraska State Historical Society, Lincoln, Nebr.
New Hampshire	New Hampshire State Library, Concord, N.H.
New Jersey	New Jersey State Library, Trenton, N.J.
New York	New York State Library, Albany, N.Y.
North Carolina	North Carolina Department of Archives and History, Raleigh, N.C.
Ohio	State Library of Ohio, Columbus, Ohio
Oregon	Oregon State Library Salem, Ore.
Pennsylvania*	NARA, Philadelphia, Pa. (Microfilm only)
Rhode Island	Rhode Island State Archives, Providence, R.I.
South Carolina	South Carolina Archives Department, Columbia, S.C.
Tennessee*	Duke University Library, Durham, N.C.
Texas*	Texas State Library, Austin, Tex.
Vermont*	Vermont State Library, Burlington, Vt.
Virginia*	Virginia State Library, Richmond, Va.
Washington* (1860, 1870)	Washington State Library, Olympia, Wash.
West Virginia* (1870)	West Virginia Department of Archives and History, Charleston, W.V.
Wisconsin	State Historical Society of Wisconsin, Madison, Wis.

* Microfilm available through the National Archives regional facilities in addition to those listed. (Chart taken from "Nonpopulation Census Schedules: Their Location," compiled by Claire Prechtel-Kluskens, 1995.)

addresses in Boston from 1853 to 1865 and had many different business partners.

1853: 92 Hanover St.

1854: 114 Hanover and 199 Hanover St.

1854: 94 Hanover St.

1855–1859: 114 Hanover

1864–1865: 109 Washington St.

Included in the information that Steele and Polito discovered in the directory listings were the following partnerships:

Welch & Higgins (1852–53)

Higgins & Pushee (1859–1860)

Higgins & Brothers (1860–61)

Higgins & Whitaker (1861)

Higgins & Collier (1862)

Higgins & Company (1863–65)

Higgins, Chandler & Company (ca. 1860–70)

If you were researching a photograph with the imprint Higgins & Whitaker, you would know the photograph was taken in 1861. Other information you collected from the image may support that conclusion. Newspapers often carried photographers' advertisements, news items about them, and obituaries.

Advertisements in newspapers generally listed the services that a photographer offered and a price schedule. Unless the newspaper you are using is indexed, such material can be difficult to locate. This is a labor-intensive search and should be saved until you exhaust all other research options. Sometimes a newspaper would run a story on a local studio, especially if someone famous visited to have a portrait taken or a new process was introduced.

Occasionally, you will find a mention of a photographer in a newspaper in a completely unexpected spot. Photographer Samuel Masury trained with one of America's first daguerreotypists, John Plumbe, whose skill with capturing images was well known. A reporter from a Providence, Rhode Island, newspaper heard that Masury opened a studio in the city and commented in an editorial on the images he took. "We have not seen any specimens of the art which we prefer to those of Mr. Masury." The date of this article establishes Masury as a photographer operating in Providence in January 1846.

The United States Newspaper Project is a special federally funded project whose goal is to create a nation-wide listing of newspapers published in each state. A central repository of newspapers in each state that is participating in the project can help you locate a newspaper for a particular area. In some localities, directories don't exist but newspapers do. If you can find a newspaper for the town your photographer lived in, you may be able to obtain a microfilm reel through your local public library. The Library of Congress, Chronicling America <**chroniclingamerica.loc.gov**> is an online resource for newspapers from 1880–1922, and it also contains a list of U.S. newspapers published from 1690 to present day.

There are other digital newspaper collections, such as Ancestry.com <**www.ancestry.com**> and GenealogyBank.com <**www.genealogybank.com**>. For more useful sites see *Everything You Need to Know About…How to Find Your Family History in Newspapers* by Lisa Louise Cooke.

Subscription books, sometimes known as mug or booster books, can be a tremendous help in finding a photographer. These books featured biographies of prominent individuals. If the photographer you are researching was well established in a locality, he may have contributed to a county or town history. These mug book sketches, often written by the person depicted, contain biographical information that can help you. A note of warning: Since the subject of the sketch was often also its author, the importance of his life and work may be exaggerated. Back up any information from a subscription book with documented facts.

Publications created for a special purpose, such as a centennial celebration, are also good resources. Such publications usually accepted advertising from local businesses and might even feature a brief history of the studio in which you are interested

Photography magazines of the period also published articles on studios and accepted advertising. By searching an index of these journals for all years a studio was operating, you may find additional information on the photographer. From an article in the *Photographic Art Journal*, Steele and Polito learned that Luther Holman Hale began his photography business on Milk Street in Boston. This information does not appear in any other source.

Federal and state census records can also assist you in the search for the dates of a photographer. Census indexes are available on the Internet, in libraries, and through search services. Use the census indexes to supply a volume and page number for a photographer's census report.

The Manchester Brothers of Providence, Rhode Island, used several different imprints during their years of business. The crossed out name represents the end of a partnership.

The search for the history of the Manchester Brothers photography imprint in Providence, Rhode Island, is an example of what research can uncover about a photographer. Following the guidelines in this chapter for identifying a photographer from an imprint and utilizing information in printed sources and online directed the research and helped piece together background information on the two brothers.

One of the first steps in researching a photographer is examining images taken by them. The imprints embossed on the images show that the company was known by several names: Manchester and Chapin, Manchester Brothers, Manchester Brothers and Angell, and Manchester Bros. No other information appears in the imprint except the names.

Two things are apparent from examining their images. First, the Manchester Brothers operated from the daguerreotype era to at least the end of the nineteenth century. Second, at least some of the images are of notable Rhode Islanders.

A search of the city directories for Providence, Rhode Island, revealed the following information:

1850–1853
Edwin H. and H.N. Manchester. Daguerrean Artist
33 Westminster St.

1853–1854
Manchesters and Chapin
19 & 33 Westminster St.

1853–1859
Manchesters and Chapin,
73 Westminster St.

1860–1862
Manchester and Brother
73 Westminster St.

1863
Manchester Brothers
73 Westminster St.

1864
Manchester Brothers
74 Westminster St.

1865
Manchester Brothers and Angell
73 Westminster St.

1866–1868
Manchester Brother & Angell
73 Westminster St.

1869–1878
Manchester Bros.
73 Westminster St.

1880
Manchester Bros.
329 Westminster St.

CASE STUDY continued next page →

In addition to business addresses, the city directory listings provided the brothers' names, Edwin and Henry N., their residential addresses, and Henry's death on 24 November 1881. Directories are also useful in tracing the development of a family. In this case, George E. Manchester joined the family business in 1878. Cross-checking the listing revealed the names of the Manchesters' partners: Joshua Chapin, a doctor, and Daniel Angell.

The next step is to take the information gleaned from the directories and look for obituaries in the local newspaper, *The Providence Evening Bulletin*. The death indexes confirm the death date on Henry N. and provide one for his brother Edwin, 20 March 1904. The obituary of Edwin includes a photograph of him, establishes him as a brother to Henry, and provides his middle initial—H. The brothers operated a daguerreotype studio in Newport, Rhode Island, in approximately 1842. At some point, Edwin opened a studio in Pawtucket, Rhode Island, and Henry started one in Providence. The George E. listed in the directories is mentioned as Henry's son.

Since Edwin's obituary states that the Manchesters were well known among the older families of Providence, the next step is to look at biographical encyclopedias. Henry Niles Manchester and Edwin Hartwell Manchester, as well as one of their partners, Joshua Chapin, are mentioned in a mug book. This biographical information establishes that they were in Providence in 1844 working with another photographer, Samuel Masury, in both Providence and Woonsocket, Rhode Island. The brothers also continued to operate a studio in Newport during the summer season.

The encyclopedia mentions that they were one of the first studios to introduce the paper print to Rhode Island, so they might be mentioned in William S. Johnson's *Nineteenth Century Photography: An Annotated Bibliography, 1839–1879* (Boston: G. K. Hall & Co., 1990). Johnson's book indexes images by photographers that appeared in nineteenth-century periodicals. One image is listed for the Manchester Brothers and one for the Manchester Brothers and Angell. Both prints appeared in *Harper's Weekly* and depict famous Rhode Islanders.

Census information on both Manchester brothers corroborated the information found in printed sources. A search of newspaper indexes at the Providence Public Library located a story about someone employed by the Manchesters and included a narrative about meeting and photographing Edgar Allan Poe.

Duplicating the printed source's search using online databases illustrates the possibilities that exist for this type of research. From Craig's Daguerreian Registry, it is learned that Edwin was a daguerreian in Providence, Rhode Island, from 1848 to 1860. A complete listing of business addresses and partnerships is part of his biography. However, the first new material for the Manchester Brothers is found in the citation for Henry Niles Manchester.

Henry was first listed as a daguerreian in 1843 at 75 Court Street, Boston, which was the address of Plumbe's Gallery. In 1846, he was listed in Providence, R.I., at 13 Westminster Street, as Manchester, Thompson & Co. In 1847, he was listed alone at 33 Market Street. Another source has placed Manchester in business with Masury and Hartshorn in Boston.

The George Eastman House database, which provides a span of dates of operation for photographers and their location, did not yield any additional information. However, the *Index to American Photographic Collections: Compiled at the International Museum of Photography at George Eastman House, 3d ed.*, edited by Andrew H. Eskin and Greg Drake (New York: G.K. Hall, 1996) tells you where to find other collections of Manchester Brothers photographs.

By taking this research and applying it to the images with the Manchester Brothers' imprint, it is possible to approximate when a specific image was taken. A carte de visite with the imprint Manchester and Chapin would have been taken sometime between 1853 and 1859, while one with the imprint Manchester Brothers and Angell would have been taken between 1865 and 1868. Any further conclusions about the photographs will have to rely on the other methods of dating an image.

Don't be misled when a photographer lists his occupation as something else, particularly in the early years of photography. Photographers often listed their occupation by the process in which they specialized. Many occupational titles were recorded for photographers, including daguerreotypist, ambrotypist, tintypist, and artist. Someone with multiple occupations would have had to pick one for the census taker, so don't be thrown if you find the right guy with the wrong job.

Special censuses or nonpopulation schedules are helpful when available (see "Special Census for Industry—1850, 1860, and 1870" on page 69). The Manufacturing or Industrial schedules from 1850 to 1880 include photographers. The purpose of these schedules was to compile information about manufacturing, mercantile, commercial, and trading businesses that had a gross product income of more than five hundred dollars.

Similar schedules taken in later years were destroyed. Information listed included the name of business or owner, amount of capital invested, and quantity and value of materials, labor, machinery, and products. Silas B. Brown, a Providence photographer, appeared in the 1860 census of industry. His product was ambrotypes; his occupation photographic artist; his worth fifteen hundred dollars, and he had five hundred picture frames and chemicals, cases, and other materials in his possession. The census also states that he had two male employees that cost him seventy-five dollars per month in wages.

ONLINE HELP

While the majority of research on photographers is still accomplished using printed materials, there are also Internet resources to help with the process. One helpful Web advantage is that card catalogs for most major libraries are online, with the number increasing daily, so you can find books to aid your search without leaving the house.

The George Eastman House, an international museum of photography, has made its database of photographers available online through a telnet database <**www.geh.org/gehdata.html**>. Libraries and archives from all over the United States contributed information. The database has information on everyone from the small-town photographer to the world-renowned. Search terms for the database include photographer, geographic location, subject, and process. Specific information relating to business addresses is not available through the database, but it will help you place a photographer in a location within a time frame. City directories are also becoming available online through a variety of sites, such as Ancestry.com.

For individuals researching daguerreotypists, the premier resource for information on American photographers from 1839 to 1860 is John S. Craig's Daguerreian Registry <**www.craigcamera.com/dag**> Craig spent decades compiling this data. Collectors, dealers, and other researchers have also submitted material for inclusion.

You can also locate information on photographers by typing the name into an online search engine, such as Google <**www. google.com**>. Consult online directories like those posted on <**www.findingphotographers. homestead.com.**> Use the listing by photographer on popular photo reunion site DeadFred.com <**www.dead-fred.com**> to find other images by the same photographer and establish a time frame for the studio. Another option is to communicate with other researchers via message boards, such as U.K. Photographers at <**www. rootsweb.ancestry.com**>.

Researching photographers is challenging, but it can also be very rewarding. If you know the name of the photographer who took that mysterious image in your collection, the material you can locate on him will supply you with one more clue.

Pat Strasser owns two identical images of the same man from two different photographers. She has two questions: Which one is the copy, and who is the man in the picture?

Photographic imprints supply part of the answer. The image on the left was taken by Orris Hunt, who states on his card that he was the successor to Harry Shepherd at 15 East Seventh St., St. Paul, Minnesota. It was quite common for one photographer to buy out another photographer's studio when he decided to retire or move on. According to *Biographies of Western Photographers* by Carl Mautz (Brownsville, Calif.: Carl Mautz Publishing, 1997), Harry Shepherd bought out the People's Photographic Gallery in 1887 and renamed it. He was a very successful African-American photographer in St. Paul, eventually owning three studios and winning an award for his work at the 1891 State Fair. He left the area around 1905, when presumably Orris Hunt purchased his East Seventh Street studio. This information suggests that the portrait of the unidentified young man was taken sometime after 1905.

The photo on the right is the copy. The photographer, Felix Schanz, was active in Fort Wayne, Indiana, in the 1920s, according to the George Eastman House database of photographers. In addition to taking new portraits of individuals, a basic part of a photographer's business was making copies of existing images.

If you are wondering about the connection between Fort Wayne and St. Paul, the answer is family. Pat Strasser's father-in-law identified

PAT STRASSER

PAT STRASSER

many of the pictures, with the exception of these two and a few others. The Strasser family lived in Fort Wayne as early as 1867, when George Strasser was born. An older stepsister of George's, Amada Hall (b. 1859), married a Danish immigrant, Edward Steade, in 1880. They moved to North Dakota and later Minneapolis, which is close to St. Paul. Pat thought this could be a portrait of Edward Steade, but given the dates of the photographer and other clues, this man is too young to be Edward. His clothing clues point to the early twentieth century: a loose-fitting jacket worn unbuttoned with a vest, knit tie, and shirt with a stand-up collar. It appears that he is wearing a false shirtfront with the tie tucked into it. Perhaps this was an attempt to dress up a more ordinary, everyday shirt. It is possible that this is a graduation picture. Given these clothing clues, the original photograph fits the time frame for Orris Hunt's business and probably dates no later than 1910.

Here's a theory as to what happened to that photograph. I suspect the man pictured is a son of Amada and Edward Steade. He had his picture taken by Orris Hunt and sent one to his grandparents. Years later, other family members wanted copies and visited Felix Schanz's studio. Somehow, these two photographs (one original and one duplicate) ended up in her father-in-law's collection. Pat Strasser is working on another lead for identification. There was another branch of the family living in Minneapolis that had a son at the right age for the portrait.

"Generally, a child will sit best if left entirely to the operator."

—COLEMAN AND REMINGTON, PHOTOGRAPHIC ARTISTS, 25 WESTMINSTER ST., PROVIDENCE (FROM THE RHODE ISLAND HISTORICAL SOCIETY)

7

Images From Birth to Death

Most family photograph collections are a diverse group of images depicting relatives, friends, and events that document an ancestor's life. Some collections record only the key moments in a person's life; others provide a photographic timeline of a person from birth to death. What exists in your photograph collection depends on how important photography was to your family.

1840
The first school photograph, the Yale Class of 1810, is taken by Samuel F.B. Morse

1868
H.M. Crider introduces photographic marriage certificates.

1947
E.H. Land discovers a one-step photo process that develops in less than a minute—the first Polaroid.

1861–1865
Mathew Brady chronicles the Civil War in photos.

1888
Kodak roll film is-invented ("You push the button—we do the rest"), popularizing candid photography.

In either case, every collection is a unique group of images similar only in the fact that they usually fall into several distinct categories: pictures of children, weddings, military service, holidays, vacations, and special occasions. Some collections contain images documenting educational milestones and even death. By looking at your family collection in terms of who and what was photographed, you'll gain an understanding of what was significant to your family.

CHILDREN

Long exposure times in the daguerreotype era made it difficult to take a good image of a fidgety child, so photographers employed contraptions and techniques to hold children still. Pictures of young children and babies may contain an expected surprise—a glimpse of the person who held the child in place for the portrait. In most cases, it is unknown whether the person hidden by a piece of draped fabric was the mother or a photographer's assistant. Date photographs of children by photographic method, photographer's imprint, clothing, and by estimating the children's age at the time of the picture.

SCHOOL

Schools have been taking photographs of their students and alumni since the first class portrait was taken in 1840. Some are group shots of children posed in classrooms or in front of the school building, while others are individual portraits. It was popular in the late nineteenth and early twentieth century to pose for a formal graduation portrait. These are recognizable because young women dressed entirely in white. The most common prop was a rolled diploma. You can locate additional school-age photographs of your ancestors in school records, class books, and twentieth-century yearbooks.

WEDDINGS

Wedding photographs in the nineteenth century do not resemble the wedding photographs of today. White gowns were generally not worn because they were an unnecessary expense. Even if a bride wore a formal white gown, she would not be photographed in it, because early cameras could not photograph bright colors in any detail. Wedding portraits usually show the married couple in regular clothes or in their traveling garments.

COLLECTION OF THE AUTHOR

Look for images of your ancestors throughout their lives. Photographing your child as an infant has always been popular.

COLLECTION OF THE AUTHOR

School portraits and graduation photos often become part of a family's photo collection.

78

PHOTO BY SCHRIEVER

Try to locate photographs of all of the marriages that took place after 1839 in your family tree.

The style of wedding portraits changed with the availability of images of royal weddings. These royal portraits could be purchased from booksellers and photographers. Victorian brides emulated the fashion and photographs of these royal couples in their own weddings. Victorian wedding albums generally include a group portrait of the participants, a static shot of the gifts, and a portrait of the bride and groom. Use the techniques explained in chapter ten to interpret the wedding images in your collection.

MILITARY SERVICE

There are photographs of military service for nearly every war in this country, including portraits of Revolutionary War patriots who lived until the age of photography. It was the Civil War, however, that created a demand for images. Soldiers would visit itinerant battlefield photographers to sit for tintype portraits they could send home to their families. Soldiers also collected photos of members of their unit and mailed them home with their letters. The quality of the image varied based on the

LIBRARY OF CONGRESS

Children of the Barker Cotton Mill School, Mobile, Alabama

The Library of Congress attributes this photo to Lewis Hine because of the photo's provenance, or history of ownership of the image.

According to *The Oxford Companion to the Photograph* edited by Robin Leman, Lewis Wickes Hine (1874-1940), a photographer and a sociologist, used a camera to highlight the social issues of his times. A former factory worker, Hine took photographs of immigrants at Ellis Island and then worked for the National Child Labor Committee (NCLC) on a campaign to end child labor in occupations not suitable for children.

This photo, taken in October 1914, was part of a collection of Hine's photographs published alongside worksite reports by the NCLC between 1910 and 1920 while the NCLC was advocating for legislation that would end child labor.

A note in the cataloging record suggests that there are more photographs and information in "the Alabama report."

It's possible that these can be found in Cornell University Library's online "Guide to the National Child Labor Committee Publications," **<http://rmc.library.cornell. edu/ead/htmldocs/KCL05242.html>**.

An NCLC caption card titles the photo "Group of children attending the mill school at Barker Cotton Mills," and identifies the school's location as Mobile, Alabama.

photographer's skill and the appearance of the soldier. In one unit, a Sergeant Taylor wrote home that he "will send you a thing that looks a little like me, but not much. Don't be frightened nor let the children get scared at it."

Battlefield scenes and portraits of officers are present in many family collections. Use care when identifying military images of the Civil War; the men depicted in the portraits may not be relatives. Booksellers and

photographers sold copies of significant events and people that soldiers or their families would buy to serve as a reminder of a particular battle.

In the years after the advent of amateur photography, soldiers and service personnel, such as military doctors, nurses, and cooks, would document their military career with photographs. One World War I nurse, Gertrude Bray, documented her travels and companions during

Study the History

Searching the words *Barker Cotton Mill* in Google Books **<books.google.com>** turns up several hits. *The History of Alabama and Dictionary of Alabama Biography by Thomas McAdory Owen and Marie Bankhead Owen* provide statistics about the mill. It was incorporated in 1900 and produced sheeting, diaper cloth, toweling, and yarns for market.

The fifty-four students (and a few teachers) depicted in this image, appear mostly clean, well-dressed, and happy.

Look closely at the front row. All but one of the children is barefoot. Only the girl on the far left wears white stockings and shoes. She's also the only one in a stylish dress with a sailor collar and a dropped waist in a contrasting fabric. Her outfit suggests that her family was in a better financial position than some of the boys on the far right in their slightly dusty shirts, rolled pants and suspenders.

Two of the children on the left look down instead of squinting at the camera, they are more intent on whatever is on the ground than the photographer.

The NCLC caption card cited on the Library of Congress Web site continues, "These children are well-kept at home, and well-directed in school. School is sanitary and well-equipped. School attendance is compulsory. Deputy in the mill acts as truant officer. If parents neglect to send children to school, they are requested to move out. The whole situation reflects the good management of the superintendent."

Identify the Children

The children in this photo appear to be grouped by age (or size) in this picture. Two women, possibly teachers, stand in the back row under the roof overhang.

While the full names of the children probably don't appear in the published report, it might be possible to identify who was enrolled at the school. One way to do this would be to track down education records for the mill school using the National Union Catalog of Manuscript Collections **<www.loc.gov/coll/nucmc>** or by contacting local archives and libraries.

When this photo was taken, it was common for employees of a factory to live in company housing, so it might be possible to match children with families mentioned in the 1910 U.S. Census for Mobile. The factory was once part of Barker Cotton Mill Village, in an area now part of Pritchard, Alabama.

Searching for Barker Cotton Mill with a date range of 1915–1990 on **<GenealogyBank.com>** turned up several articles relating to reunions held by folks who once worked at the factory. These accounts are another lead to identifying the children.

One of the women in the back row is likely Miss Bessie Rencher. According to her obituary in the *Mobile Register*, (January 27, 1973), Miss Rencher began teaching at the mill in 1912, and, together with a Miss Daphne Roberts, taught children during the day and ran a night school for their parents.

the war in her photograph albums. Family collections usually contain at least some pictorial material relating to family military service.

Images of men in uniform offer evidence of an ancestor's military service. Look at uniforms, insignias, and the photographer's identification to date and piece together information regarding rank or campaigns. Learn techniques for understanding your military images in chapter ten.

PHOTOGRAPHS AVAILABLE DURING THE CIVIL WAR, 1861–1865

- Daguerreotypes

- Ambrotypes

- Tintypes

- *Cartes de visite*

HOLIDAYS

Families began photographing holiday celebrations when candid photography became available in the late nineteenth century. Holiday pictures include informal family scenes and meals, as well as photographic cards exchanged to commemorate the occasion. Photographic cards sometimes provide you with the names of close friends of the family. Those family friends may also have images of your family in their collections.

Photographic holiday greetings have been around since photography's early beginnings in the 1840s. Individuals often sent pictures of themselves or their children to friends and relatives with a holiday greeting written on the back; they also ordered pictures with a preprinted message, just as we do today. If your family has been sending and receiving cards for a number of years—or even generations—you've probably accumulated quite a collection. Rather than discard these images because they are not of your relatives, here are a few ideas on what to do with them after the holiday is over.

Add Them to Your Collection

These photographic greetings capture a family at a given moment in time. While most included a standard greeting such as "Happy New Year," the person sending the picture occasionally wrote a year and at least a first name. In the case of unidentified nineteenth-century images, a first name and a date, combined with a photographer's imprint, can help you add the surname and identify the person in the picture. Preprinted cards popular in the twentieth century usually just gave the surname of the family sending it, so your job is to add the first names to the family group. If you receive any undated photo greetings this holiday season, label each one on the back with the full name of the people depicted and the year. Organize all these photo cards by surname or holiday in your family files and preserve a piece of your heritage for future generations.

The Friendship Connection

A friend of mine inherited a large box of old mementos, including several decades' worth of photographic cards. If you find yourself with a similar collection, don't discard them because they aren't your family—think of them as an opportunity. Connect with your family's past friendships; renew the link and discover new family information. Here are a couple of ideas.

- If you still know the people in the portrait, present the family with the collection and give back their photographic heritage. I doubt they kept a copy for themselves.

- Track down the family friends depicted in the photos and ask if they have any pictures of your relatives.

- Research the individuals in the pictures and add the information to your genealogy. The photos can help illustrate your family history.

COLLECTION OF THE AUTHOR

Holiday card, circa 1880s.

Tell a Story

Any photograph can trigger memories that provide relatives with a chance to tell a story from the past, but pictures from special occasions can be particularly effective, since friends and family were gathered together in good cheer. Start an informal interview with a simple question—ask family members what they were thinking when they had their holiday picture taken. Was it taken at a studio with all the children dressed identically, on a vacation, or does it show a spontaneous moment? Then ask them to relate their holiday traditions. You'll add new details to your family history and end up with an oral history about the way your family celebrated the holidays.

RELIGIOUS OCCASIONS

A photograph of a young girl dressed in white or a boy with a white bow on his arm is probably a portrait from a religious occasion, such as a child's First Communion or Confirmation. Such pictures document your ancestor's participation in a religious community and open new opportunities for family research.

Examine costume details to establish a time frame for the image. Basic clothing styles reflect when the picture was taken, such as leg-of-mutton sleeves in the 1890s or the heavy chain jewelry of the 1870s. Costumes can also reflect the order to which those individuals belonged— look for photographs of people in religious garb, such as altar boys, priests, and nuns.

First Communion or Confirmation portraits often contain other props, such as Bibles, candles, flowers, and religious symbols. These items will vary depending on the denomination of the event depicted. The presence of a recognizable religious symbol or ceremonial prop is a clue worth deciphering. It can be a timesaver in your search for written or printed documents.

VACATIONS AND RECREATION

Our ancestors used photography to help them remember special events, including picnics, family outings, sporting events, and vacations. People often created albums of images they had taken or pictures they purchased to share with family later. These photographs capture how your ancestors spent their free time.

COLLECTION OF THE AUTHOR

Photographs of religious events like this First Communion portrait can lead to the discovery of new historical documents concerning your family, c.1870.

LYNN BETLOCK

Postmortem photos can establish a death date in the absence of a vital record.

POSTMORTEM

Postmortem or memorial photography was a common way of documenting a member of the family. The tradition of memorializing the dead with an image has a long history that predates photography—wealthy families had portraits painted of deceased family members. When photography became available, it gradually replaced the painted postmortem portrait and leveled the economic playing field—now it was possible for almost anyone to have an image of a deceased family member taken. Memorial photographs were most commonly taken of children who died before their parents could have a portrait painted. Postmortem images can be quite disturbing if you are not prepared to see a grieving mother holding her dead infant.

Some photographers who specialized in postmortem photography learned techniques to capture a good quality image. Children might be photographed sitting on a parent's lap, in a coffin, or resting peacefully. Adults photographed after death could also be found in a variety of poses. It is not unusual to find a photograph of an open casket in a living room with images propped up in the casket.

Photographs of the deceased sometimes were incorporated into a tombstone design. Photos on a tombstone are extremely rare, but they do exist.

With the popularity of the card photograph, preprinted black memorial cards became part of the funeral to serve as a remembrance of the individual who had passed on. Copies of previously taken photos could also be ordered and mounted to a black card stock or to a card with a black border.

Certain compositional elements, such as the inclusion of props can date a memorial image. For instance, in the 1860s, it was popular to photograph deceased infants in their baby carriages.

Photographic trends in postmortem photography can also date an image. Grave-side or spirit images that included "ghostly" portraits of the deceased when they were alive superimposed over a coffin were common in the late nineteenth century.

Death could also be alluded to in a photograph. Individuals holding photographs or wearing photographic jewelry may be an indication of someone not present, either due to death or absence.

RESOURCES ON POSTMORTEM PHOTOGRAPHY

Secure the Shadow: Death and Photography in America by Jay Ruby (Cambridge: MIT Press, 1995).

Sleeping Beauty: Memorial Photography in America by Stanley B. Burns (Altadena, Calif.: Twelvetrees Press, 1990).

SPOTTING A MOURNING PHOTO

- During the 1860s, widows generally wore black clothing including undersleeves and black crape drapery for the first year. In the second year of mourning, some white could be introduced in undersleeves and collars

- Watch for accessories: Accessories also reflected mourning, such as jewelry made from jet (or cheaper black glass), as well as pieces that incorporate human hair. While not all jewelry that features hair represents a deceased person, it was a popular way to honor the memory of the dead. Rings, pins, and lockets with typical mourning symbols, such as grave-side scenes or weeping willows, indicate a mourning piece. Men often wore mourning rings, given out as tokens at funerals.

- The stages of mourning dictated a woman's attire. For instance, a woman in full mourning for a husband would wear a black dress with dark collars and cuffs. Dark black fabric devoid of any gloss or shine was the style. Her hat would be draped in black crape and a veil.

PHOTOGRAPHS USUALLY FOUND IN FAMILY COLLECTIONS

Children

- Infant portrait
- Mother and child
- Posed with siblings
- Posed with family pet
- Individual portrait

Weddings

- Single portrait of bride and groom together
- Matching portraits of the bride and groom
- Group portrait of the wedding party
- Photograph of the gifts
- Engagement portrait

- Candid photographs of the event
- Anniversary photo

Military Service

- Portraits of individuals in uniform
- Regimental photographs
- War scenes
- Photo albums of wartime activities
- Photographs of other service personnel

School

- Student portraits
- Class photos
- Graduation pictures

- Informal photographs of class activities

Holidays and Special Events

- New Year's cards
- Christmas cards
- Parades
- Social activities
- Vacations and recreation

Occupational Images

- Ancestors at work
- Group portrait of co-workers

Membership in an Organization

- Posed in fraternal uniforms
- Group portraits of member events

"To consider photography a mere mechanical art is a great mistake... photography to be successful requires expensive apparatus..."

— COLEMAN AND REMINGTON, PHOTOGRAPHIC ARTISTS, 25 WESTMINSTER ST., PROVIDENCE (FROM THE RHODE ISLAND HISTORICAL SOCIETY)

8

Looking for Clues

While the type of photograph may place the image in a time period, the internal clues can narrow it down to a specific date. By carefully examining all the details present in a picture and recording them on a worksheet, you can discover the story of a photograph. In a portrait, facial characteristics can help you identify an image while the choice of props and backgrounds provide insight into the personality of the sitter.

1840s
The appearance of the first painted backdrop in a photograph.

1900
There are 10,000 automobiles in the United States; by 1910 the number had grown to half a million, due to the more than 240 car manufacturers producing vehicles.

1960
The American Flag appears for the first time as it does today, with fifty stars.

1879
Thomas Edison produces the first incandescent light bulb; by 1930, most homes have electric lighting.

1925–1935
Zigzag patterns and vertical lines create dramatic effect on jazz-age, Art Deco buildings.

Photographs of interior or exterior scenes contain many items that can help you date an image. For instance, to date an interior scene, you can research the decorative details. The presence or absence of certain technological details, such as light fixtures, trolley lines, and paved streets can date exterior shots. If a street scene has electric lights, for example, then you can research when lighting was installed in that part of town. Dating the style of architecture can also place the image in a time frame. The easiest detail to research in a street scene is signage. For some searches, it may be necessary to correspond with relatives or to contact experts on the subject to help you establish a date.

FAMILY RESEMBLANCES

Probably the most difficult technique involved in photo identification is identifying and grouping people by facial characteristics. In some families, there may be a distinguishing characteristic, such as a mole that appears in a particular part of the face in several family members, or a distinctive shape of the eyes or nose. Hopefully your collection of photographs contains some

> **DETAILS TO LOOK FOR IN AN IMAGE**
>
> - Facial characteristics
> - Props
> - Architecture
> - Technological details (streetlights, trolleys, etc.)
> - Signage

identified images, so that you can begin to group them by family facial attributes.

Criminal investigators use facial characteristics to identify suspects, and you can use some of their techniques to try to identify people in family photographs. Police identification specialists use a standard list of characteristics to help create a composite. You will be attempting to do just that. Inspect the faces in your photographs and create a table of unique aspects to look for.

GRANT EMISON

Use caution when comparing facial characteristics: a person's face changes over time.

How do you identify a family photograph if you don't even know what side of the family the image belongs to? The answer is to look for physical features that distinguish one side from the other. In Rita Werner's case, the striking resemblance between two women in her photograph collection leaves no doubt to a family relationship. At age seventy-six, Grandmother Bernice (on the right) would look just like her unidentified ancestor (on the left) if she were wearing a daycap. With the family line identified, Rita wants to know who is in the first photograph and when it was taken.

The photographer's imprint, C.H. Scofield of Utica, New York, is one clue. An online search reveals that a C.H. Scofield took stereoscopic pictures of Utica circa 1866 to 1900. You can view them on the Library of Congress American Memory Web site at **<memory.loc.gov>**. A photographer named C.H. Scofield (alternate spelling, Scholfield) also appears in Utica city directories from 1874 to at least 1889. He bragged in one city directory advertisement that he was the only photographer in Utica with rooms on the first floor. In the days before flash photography, natural light was an important component in taking portraits, so most studios were on the top floor. Due to having a studio accessible without climbing stairs, he probably attracted an older clientele—much like the woman on the left.

It is possible to narrow the time period of the photograph based on its physical characteristics. Yellow cards with rounded corners were popular for photographs between 1871 and 1874, according to William C. Darrah's *Cartes de Visite in Nineteenth Century Photography*. The woman on the left is wearing a daycap with ruffles on the sides, an indication of her conservative approach to fashion. Women's magazines of the nineteenth century suggested that only young women should dress fashionably because older, married women had other concerns—those of home and family. But no matter how old-fashioned a woman's dress, attention to detail showed her awareness of current fashion. In this image, the woman wears a neck ribbon with a charm attached, as was the fashion in the 1870s. Her black dress, while simple in design, features some trim around the wrists

RITA WERNER

and at the end of the jacket. The presence of the neck ribbon and the style of photograph suggest this image was taken in the early 1870s.

Werner suspects this woman is her fourth-great-grandmother, the grandmother of Thomas R. Connor (1848–1934). Connor was born in Ireland and immigrated to the United States in 1870. According to family legend, either Connor's maternal or paternal grandmother raised him after his father, a merchant seaman, died at sea. It is possible that his grandmother immigrated with him, but this photograph might be the only evidence. A family photograph album does list a Mrs. E. Connor in the index. This mention could refer to the woman in the image and would support the family story. Werner also knows of an Elizabeth Connor (1814–1903) buried in a Utica cemetery, and she is trying to ascertain her origins.

Rita Werner may never be able to identify the woman in the left-hand photo, but one thing is certain—she is a relative. A quick glance at the two photographs she submitted leaves no doubt about it.

Relatives can be very helpful with facial identification. If any relatives from the unidentified subject's generation are still living, you might want to enlist their help. They may recognize the individual in the photograph. Even if the name eludes them, they may be able to offer additional clues. The props and background in the image may aid your relatives in identifying the person in the photograph.

PHYSICAL CHARACTERISTICS TO EXAMINE

In particular, it is helpful to look at:

- Shape of face: oval, heart shaped, round, square

- Eyes (shape, position, color, size)

- Nose and nostrils (shape, size)

- Ears (shape, size, position on head, length)

- Hair pattern (baldness, widow's peaks)

- Eyebrows (size, shape)

- Moles

- Teeth

Trace a photocopy of a family portrait, reduce it to the scale of the photo you are trying to identify, and compare jaws, ears, and facial shape. This can also be done by scanning an image and manipulating it using photo-editing software. Be careful with this method of identification, though—a person's face changes with age and weight tends to fluctuate.

Lay your identified family photos out in a timeline for each person. Compare your unidentified images to the timelines. Noticing similar noses, eyes, or cheekbones can establish a family connection. Those images that defy identification will require further research.

When you create your photographic timeline, use photocopies of the images so you can retain the layout of the collection as arranged by the original owner. Re-examining the photographs in the context in which they were given to you can also help to identify individuals.

CASE STUDY: **CELEBRITY LOOK-ALIKE**

COLLECTION OF THE AUTHOR
Unidentified man

LIBRARY OF CONGRESS
Walt Whitman

Walt Whitman is likely one of the most photographed men of the nineteenth century. In the mid-1850s, he posed for a portrait to include in his book *The Leaves of Grass*. Instead of wearing a suit, Whitman wore an open-necked work shirt and a hat and posed with his hand on one hip.

He continued to pose for portraits until shortly before his death. At a recent photo show, I spotted this cabinet card of an older man with a full beard and thought, *doesn't he look like Walt Whitman*. Could it be him? Here's how to compare faces.

Examine the features—eyes, nose, mouth and even hairline. This man looks a lot like Whitman with two exceptions—his eyebrows and the spacing between brow and eye. This man's eyebrows are light and barely visible. Throughout his life, Whitman had strong brows even as a very elderly man.

When you think you own a previously unknown image of a famous person, take a few minutes to compare facial features and add up the photo facts. In most cases, it will just be a look-alike.

Facial comparison is all about the details. Computer models that claim to accurately compare faces range from Google's Picasa and Google Images to iPhoto for the Mac. So how does it work?

Basically, your face is composed of eighty various features that can be matched to another person or a photo of a person. In general this software looks for the distance between the eyes, the shape of the nose, cheekbones, and jaw line and whether or not a person has deep-set eyes.

The best results are achieved when both faces are looking directly into the camera. Obviously this doesn't always happen with family photos, which often have individuals photographed at various angles in addition to image quality issues. It is possible to end up with photo matches for relatives or those individuals who just look like someone else.

On television, police investigation shows use facial recognition to catch criminals, but in real life, accuracy is not even close to 100 percent. A new program, called Faceoff, lets you compare two photos side by side. Learn more at **<www. visualfacerecognition.com>**.

PROPS AND BACKDROPS

Studio photographers placed their customers in a deliberate setting using props and backdrops. Common props were toys, books, flowers, drapery, and columns. Their purpose was to add interest to the picture. People could also supply their own props, and in some cases, these can be significant. A woman posed in mourning clothes with a man's photograph may be including her deceased husband in the portrait. Occupational portraits sometimes contain clues regarding the subject's employment.

Painted backdrops first appeared in photographs in the 1840s, coinciding with the popularity of the daguerreotype. Backdrops provided the context for the props. Studios employed artists to create backdrops similar to the ones used in the theater. With the appropriate props, a visit to the photographer could transport customers into another world. Frontier scenes, landscapes, and architecture were popular backdrops in nineteenth-century images. Creative photographers would set props against an appropriate background painting. The backdrop could even substitute for actual props and make it appear that people were posing with items that are actually only painted surfaces, such as architectural details like balustrades. People could pose with bicycles in front of a landscape or appear to be riding in a car in an outdoor setting.

The choice of props and backdrops are not just useful for dating an image, but can provide clues to the character and personality of your ancestors. People could manipulate the setting of a photograph to create a sense

COLLECTION OF THE AUTHOR

Many photo studios used theatrical backdrops and props in their photographs. Note the hay in the foreground in this 1888 photo.

VALERIE MORAN

Dating this photograph didn't require examining clothing details or finding out when the photographer was in business. The evidence was so obvious that it was easy to overlook. Sometimes the smallest details immediately date a photograph—in this case, the details are the flags. By simply counting the number of stars, I discovered the picture was taken within a four-year time frame—4 July 1908, to 3 January 1912.

Twenty-seven versions of Old Glory have been used since the Stars and Stripes became official on 14 June 1777. Several versions of the American flag have flown since the advent of photography in 1839—so if you see one in a picture, count the stars and add up the rest of the clues to see if the date fits.

Valerie Moran thought the people in this picture were her ancestors, but she wasn't sure. Once you have a time frame for a picture, see if other clues can narrow it down. Everyone in this photograph wears summer attire—most of the women have on lightweight, white summer dresses or shirts, while the men pose without jackets. The women's attire—pouched-front blouses, wide belts, and long, straight skirts—fits the time period for the flags, as does

the Gibson Girl hairstyle, in which the hair is pulled into a bun on top of the women's heads. Just the combination of the women's clothing and the date of the flag is enough to date this picture between 1908 and 1912.

But when identifying a photograph, I usually try to narrow the time frame even further. In this case, the history of the flag might date the picture to a day. Oklahoma joined the Union on 16 November 1907, but the new flag didn't debut until 4 July 1908. The summer attire and new flag suggest that these people were celebrating a patriotic holiday, maybe the introduction of the new flag on Independence Day.

Based on her family data and continuing research, Moran suspects the photograph was taken in 1912. She believes the young man on the right is Clifford John Caminade (b. 1885), who would have been twenty-seven years old that year, and the older man on the left is his father, Louis Cass Caminade (b. 1852). Their ages, appearance, and date of the photo all support this conclusion.

Interior scenes should be as carefully examined as outdoor scenes. The artifacts in the picture may be family heirlooms or a new purchase. Family-owned luxury items, such as cameras, typewriters, binoculars, cars, and bicycles are clues to both the time period and the people pictured with them.

If you are unable to date an artifact by consulting reference books, an antique dealer can provide expertise or direct you to a collector who may be able to help. A curator at a local historical society or museum may also be a good resource.

The following should be consulted when trying to date an artifact:

• Reference books

• Antique dealers

• Collectors

• Local historical societies or museums

• Family members

of fantasy or comedy. They could have their photograph taken while miming an activity using materials they brought with them or ones the photographer had on hand. Young men in the late nineteenth century liked to be portrayed as fun-loving. Portraits often show them clowning for the camera.

INTERNAL INFORMATION

Dating and identifying exterior scenes is not a subjective process; you will be able to date many of the visible details through library research. Use a magnifying glass to examine the image for particular items that can be dated, such as business signs and architectural and technological elements. Each one of these details can be researched further and provide irrefutable evidence of a time period.

Signage can be verified by consulting city directories. This will tell you when a company was in business and where it was located.

Architectural details can be researched by consulting photographs, books, and maps. You can compare your image to other street scenes of the same location. By consulting a reference book on architecture, you can establish when a particular style was popular. Maps often illustrate when a neighborhood was developed.

Technological elements can be the final clue to dating an image. For example, the condition of a street may be a clue. Many local histories mention when paving was introduced. They may also provide dates for the installation of gas and electric lights. The presence of telegraph lines, railroad tracks, fire hydrants, and bridges can also be dated.

JANE SCHWERDTFEGER

Architectural details and clothing clues can help date exterior photographs, c.1910.

This unusual shop on the waterfront in Providence, Rhode Island, sold an eclectic mix of services and goods for mariners. Customers could buy secondhand clothing, boats, boat hardware, purchase railroad tickets for travel, or store their furniture "for fifty cents a week."

You can tell much about the store simply by looking at its exterior:

1. A crude painting of Jack the Ripper, complete with a bloody knife, adorns the facade.

2. On the far right of the building is a collection of advertising symbols for illiterate patrons—an anchor, a set of oarlocks, and a trio of oars.

3. The universal sign for a pawn shop (three connected balls) is prominently displayed, and this service would have been a draw for sailors.

Each one of the details in this photo, for instance, the pawnshop symbol and Jack the Ripper, can be researched using online search engines. Find more about the owner, Burnett S.W. Bragunn, in genealogical databases. The Curiosity Shop was demolished circa 1890.

BRAGUNN'S "Curiosity Shop" South main St

Burnett S.W. Bragunn Co's Curiosity Shop, South Main Street, Providence c.1890

COLLECTION OF THE AUTHOR

Written on the front of this Real photo postcard is "Maison Sackett. 37 Arlington Ave., Providence, R.I." On the back is a larger story.

"October 11, 1909

Many thanks for the 'Pictures' and your 'notes.' I suppose we must believe it all 'for we read it in' *The Times Democrat*. How do you like our picture? A 'smart feller' took it unknown and then brought round to sell. Your window looks a little empty this year. Wish you could have filled it again, you & Miss Katie. Regards to all G.O.S."

Let's see how the details add up.

- The postcard is postmarked October 11, 1909 3:30 P.M.

- It is addressed to Miss Marie L. Bres, 630 Pine St., New Orleans, La. Who is she?

- *The Times Democrat* newspaper of New Orleans merged with the Picayune in 1914. It is currently unknown what news was conveyed to the family on Arlington Ave.

- A quick search of Ancestry.com <ancestry.com> using the address from the front of the post card identified G.O.S. as George Olney Sackett, born in Brooklyn, N.Y. on November 12, 1863, and died on October 6, 1930 in Providence, RI. He was married to Anna Josephine Benson (1867–1951). Providence historic preservation literature identifies 37 Arlington St. as the George & Anna Sackett House. The Sacketts likely built this Dutch Colonial style house.

COLLECTION OF THE AUTHOR

- Another census search located Marie L. Bres, who was 37 in the 1910 census. She was born in Louisiana in 1873 and lived with her sister Selina E. (Bres) Gregory and Selina's husband, Wallace Gregory, along with their children. Also in the household is the Miss Katie referred to in the caption. She was Katharin Bres, age 49 in 1910.

This research only begins to tell the story between the two families, but it's a start. Every photo tells a tale. In this case, there are still questions to answer: Why did Marie and Katie spend the summer in Providence and how are the families acquainted?

The "smart feller" who took the image, was a roving photographer who traveled the neighborhood taking pictures of residences hoping to sell the views to the owners. In this case he was successful.

© RHODE ISLAND HISTORICAL SOCIETY

In this street scene of Providence, Rhode Island, two elderly gentlemen rest on the doorstep of a building. A brief penciled caption on the reverse side of the image reads "Charles St." There are a few business signs in the image that may help date it.

The internal details help narrow down the time period of the photo. The presence of trolley tracks, telephone lines, and cobblestone streets suggest that the photograph was taken after 1894. A history of the city of Providence verifies that telephone service was introduced in the city in 1881. The streets were laid with cobblestones between 1864 and 1880. Another clue to the time period are the electric trolley tracks, which were in existence from 1892 to 1994. In 1910, this particular type of trolley support pole was replaced.

A good next step is to research the four signs that appear in the photograph. The most easily read sign is

for the Boston Dye House. City directory research for 1894–1910 does not reveal any dye houses of that name. The only other two businesses present in the image are a barbershop and a cigar store, but both are without names. Several possibilities are listed in the 1894–1910 business directories for Providence, Rhode Island.

The last sign is in Yiddish. It took consultation with several individuals before the sign was deciphered. The sign refers to a business that sells books and religious articles.

A final date for the photograph is derived from information in a house directory, which is arranged by street address and lists who lived or worked at any given address. This showed that for the period 1894–1910 only one dyer, an Israel Levy, lived on the right street. He was in business from 1895 to 1897. The only year both a cigar shop and a barbershop operated in close vicinity was 1896.

FINDING ANSWERS

Each step in the photo identification process—talking with relatives, researching the photographer, listing internal clues, dating costumes—requires a certain familiarity with library or online research. When identifying old photographs, you'll use those techniques two basic ways—to research clues and access resources. Researching clues you find in images may mean looking at a book, talking with an expert, or searching online.

One of the best places to access resources is a library, either the brick and mortar variety or virtual ones online. Libraries, public and private, are great places to connect with resources—not just books but knowledgeable people and researchers. You may find yourself sleuthing for facts in an academic library, talking to a fellow researcher at a local historical society, using the special services offered by a public library, or hunting for answers online. Unless you live around the corner from a library like I do, you'll also want to build a home library of frequently consulted books and maintain subscriptions to online databases.

PUBLIC LIBRARIES

Regardless of what you're looking for, the local public library can be a very helpful first stop. The reference department, periodical department, and local history collection all have resources you'll want to consult.

Working With Reference Staff

Reference librarians are trained to conduct interviews to help them identify what materials in their holdings can help answer a patron's question. Getting a question answered is a matter of knowing how to ask one.

- Ask a specific question.
- Be organized.
- Discover what online resources are available for in-library use and if any can be used from home.
- Ask about other libraries in the area.
- Find out about local history resources.

If you are looking for information outside of your local area, you may be directed to The American Library Association's Directory of Libraries. It is primarily an index to libraries located in the United States, but it also includes material on Canada and Mexico. Each citation provides a brief description of the library, including departments, special services, and any special collections they maintain. This list includes private as well as public libraries. Another option is to search online for libraries in the area in which your ancestors lived.

Interlibrary Loan

If you discover that a resource you need is located at another library, a librarian may be able to obtain it via interlibrary loan. Most public libraries and many academic libraries participate in this co-operative loaning arrangement. There is an occasional charge for interlibrary loan or conditions attached, such as the lending library may require that the material stay in your library.

HELPFUL RESOURCES

The contents of reference departments vary from library to library, but you can count on even small libraries to have a good-quality encyclopedia and dictionary. These two tools enable you to learn more about an unfamiliar term found on the back of a picture.

Encyclopedias

The standard reference source is the multivolume Encyclopaedia Britannica, because of the in-depth information it offers on specific topics. It has two indexes—macropedia and micropedia. You can search this set online at **<www.britannica.com>.**

Dictionaries

A good dictionary is a valuable resource. Everyone should either own one or have access to one online or through a library. The premier source of information on the English language is the *Oxford English Dictionary*, 2d ed., 20 vols. (New York: Oxford University Press, 1989), **<www.oed.com>**. This multi-volume wonder tells you the history of a word and how its meaning may have changed over time. It can be used to look up unfamiliar words and phrases encountered when researching photographs.

SPECIAL LIBRARIES

While most public libraries have a local history collection, you may want to visit a special library. An archive or special collection usually refers to an institution or department that collects manuscripts, photographs, books, and other materials on a specific subject. Major genealogical libraries fall into the category of special libraries.

Archives and special libraries have strict rules for the use of their collections. For example, most archives require you to place personal materials, such as handbags and briefcases in lockers. Generally, you should only bring in the materials you actually need for the research you are currently undertaking. Pencils are required—no pens. You will also be asked for identification. They may even have you fill out a form asking about the resources that you have already consulted so they can suggest appropriate materials in their collection.

Some archives and special collections specialize in historic photographs. You can find a list of these institutions by consulting the American Library Association's

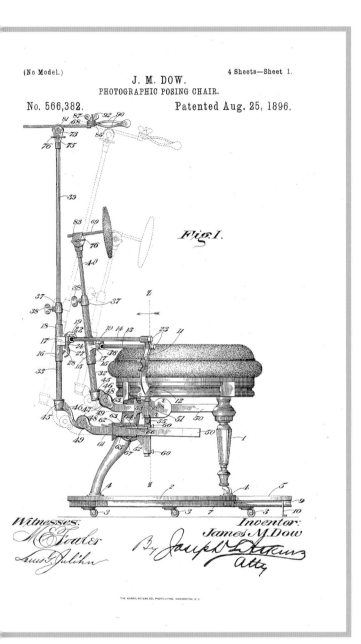

Improvement to the Photographic Posing-Chair Patent number: 566382. Filing date: Mar 14, 1895. Issue date: Aug 25, 1896. Invented by James Dow.

Directory of Libraries and the American Association of Museum's Museum Directory.

Patent and Trademark Deposit Libraries

Another type of special library is a patent deposit facility. When inventors want assurance that their invention will be protected, they register it with the United States Patent Office. These patents are public information and are stored at deposit libraries across the country.

Many early photographers patented their improvements to photographic processes. If you've found a photographer's advertisement that states they use a particular process, a patent search can help you date the image. Some photographers' imprints include a patent number. Props could also be registered with the patent office. Because each patent contains a drawing of the invention, consulting the patent records may also help date the photograph.

Full patent records are available on Google <google.com>. On the homepage, select the drop down menu and then "Even More." Click the Patent link to go to a search page for that collection. For instance, a search for *photographic headrest* results in a number of hits. See the photo of a patent in this chapter. You can

---

REFERENCES

- Costume encyclopedias
- Antique manuals
- Card catalogs
- Online resources
- Periodicals
- Indexes to various magazines and newspapers
- Copies of magazines and newspapers
- Local history collections
- Photographs
- Maps
- Published histories of the area

narrow your search by defining it using the menu on the left hand side of the page.

RESEARCH RESOURCES ONLINE

Not all of your research will be done in a traditional library setting. Online searching is convenient, and with more material available online everyday, there's no reason not to use these resources. Many academic institutions subscribe to databases, encyclopedias, and other basic reference tools that you can use from the comfort of your desk chair.

Search Engines

Use a general search engine like Google **<google.com>** or Bing **<bing.com>** to search for information on any detail present in your photographs, including the photographer's name. Be as specific as possible to limit the number of hits. Many of the leading sites also have image search engines to help you hunt for family pictures.

Online Catalogs

A good research strategy is to consult the online card catalog of the largest library in your state or a nearby state to create a bibliography of print and online resources for the topic you're researching. Then ask your local reference librarian to try to get relevant materials via interlibrary loan.

Local historical societies are slowly creating their own Web sites. While the content of these sites varies, they generally tell you how to contact the society, outline their collections, and post their hours. Some of the larger historical societies have guides for their collections as part of their site. Read their rules and regulations carefully, as not all accept queries to perform research.

E-mail

You can also use your computer to communicate with others. E-mail enables you to correspond with collectors, organizations, and other family members. For instance, you may discover that a book you have been unable to obtain is available from an organization specializing in the topic.

Use online message boards to query other researchers to see if they might have your missing information. Find the appropriate message board for your topic with organizational sites such as Cyndi's List **<www.cyndislist.com>** or by using those on Ancestry.com **<ancestry.com>**.

BUILDING A HOME LIBRARY

If you have a large family photograph collection, you will want to build a home library that you can refer to as needed. Basic volumes should include a guide to photographic processes, a general history of photography, an overview of costume history, a genealogical research guide, and a printed family genealogy (if one exists). If your photograph collection has mostly one type of image, such as daguerreotypes, you might want to purchase books on that topic. Online book libraries, such as Google Books **<books.google.com>** and the Internet Archive **<www.archive.org>** make it easy to build a research library.

I keep the books in the bibliography on page 101 on the shelf next to my desk for easy reference. I own a lot of books on specialized topics, but they're used infrequently compared to the ones on this list. Keeping up with new publications means searching online book retailers, reading *Library Journal* (a weekly publication of the American Library Association), and making regular visits to bookstores (new and used). Since space is an issue at my house and probably yours, it's important to buy only what you'll actually use. The rest I borrow through my public library. The reference department is staffed by wonderful librarians who try to find the books and articles I need through interlibrary loan from libraries all over the country. Ask your reference staff about its interlibrary loan policies. This service can help you locate the resources you need to research that unidentified photograph.

BIBLIOGRAPHY

Care and Identification of 19th-Century Photographic Prints by James M. Reilly (Rochester, N.Y.: Eastman Kodak Co., 1986). If you have a question about the type of paper photograph you own, just look it up on the pull out chart that accompanies this book. The text can teach you about the technical aspects of the picture.

Collector's Guide to Early Photographs, 2d ed. by O. Henry Mace (Iola, Wis.: Krause Publications, 1999). This slim volume can tell you just about everything you need to know about nineteenth-century photographs.

Dressed for the Photographer: Ordinary Americans and Fashion 1840–1900 by Joan L. Severa (Kent, Ohio: Kent State University Press, 1995). This is a decade-by-decade look at American fashion in photographs. Each chapter begins with an overview of styles for men, women, and children, followed by analysis of individual images for costume details.

The Genealogist's Address Book, 6th ed., by-Elizabeth Petty Bentley (Baltimore: Genealogical Publishing Co., 2009). This is a handy reference when I need to know if a local historical society has information on a particular photographer. It contains addresses for federal and state government resources and local historical resources, so I can easily find the repository or society who might have the information I need.

Unpuzzling Your Past: A Basic Guide to Genealogy by Emily Anne Croom (Baltimore: Genealogical Publishing Co., 2010). Basic, easy-to-understand information on tracing your family tree.

Victorian Costume for Ladies, 1860–1900 by Linda Setnik (Atglen, Pa.: Schiffer Publishing, 2012). Setnik examines nineteenth-century fashion, breaking it down by topics ranging from sports attire to eveningwear. This book is intended for costume collectors, but you'll find lots of interesting information on what women wore during those forty years.

Uniforms, fancy dresses, and articles of ladies [sic] attire can be sent to the studio, where dressing rooms, fitted with every convenience, are provided for the use of visitors."

—COLEMAN AND REMINGTON, PHOTO-
GRAPHIC ARTISTS, 25 WESTMINSTER ST.,
PROVIDENCE (FROM THE RHODE ISLAND
HISTORICAL SOCIETY)

9

Identifying Costume

Costumes can be extremely useful when dating and interpreting a photograph. A style of hat or the way a woman wears her hair can assign a date to an unidentified image. However, you need to be careful when dating clothing. It's very easy to make a mistake, so always double check your conclusions by looking at other images from the same time period, either in photos you've already dated or in books.

1840s
It is popular for women to wear fingerless gloves, gold watches on long chains, caps, bonnets, and bracelets made out of ribbon; men wear dark-colored neckties tied in a horizontal bow knot.

1870s
Women wear apron-like overskirts with bustles; men wear fur hats and coats.

1890s
Women wear feather boas and carry large fans and parasols; men have short haircuts with large mustaches.

1860s
Women wear hoop skirts; men wear long, over-large sack coats.

1880s
Muffs and lots of jewelry are worn by women; men sport narrow trousers with no creases.

To interpret an image using clothing, you need to be aware of the details in the costume. Not only what is being worn is important, but also how it is worn. The lack of a particular accessory or the fit of a dress can help you draw conclusions about the wearer. For example, if the fabric is different in the bodice and skirt of a woman's dress, she may be wearing parts of two different dresses. This detail reveals that the woman tried to be fashionable, even though economics prevented it.

Costumes can also be deceptive. In some tourist locations, you can have your photograph taken in period clothing. A friend of mine has a tintype of himself in a Civil War uniform. Not only was the nineteenth-century process copied, but the clothing as well. In a family photograph collection, it would be easy to mis-identify both the person and the time period of this image based solely on costume interpretation.

Dressing for a photograph was an important part of having a portrait taken. The images in family collections generally show relatives wearing their finest clothing. In order for their patrons to look their best in a studio portrait, some photographers lent clothing and accessories. Popular magazines such as *Godey's Lady's Book* advised women how to dress for portraits.

The basic elements of women's clothing remained the same during the nineteenth and early twentieth century regardless of economic status. Women almost always appear in dresses. The details of the garment—the bodice, neckline, sleeves, and skirt—can help date the photo. Accessories were a necessary part of a well-dressed woman's costume. These could include gloves, jewelry, and bonnets or hats. The variety and style of these accessories varied from decade to decade, but women's essential costume details remained much the same until the early twentieth century.

You will see little variation in men's clothing over the nineteenth and early twentieth centuries. A man's dress outfit generally consisted of a coat, shirt, trousers, tie, and possibly a vest. The style of men's hats and vests and the color or pattern of their shirts changed over time. Men's work clothes consisted of a collarless shirt, no tie, pants, suspenders, and possibly a vest.

Children's clothing for the most part resembled adult dress in the nineteenth and early twentieth century. Babies of both sexes wore long dresses with the length and details dictated by fashion. Toddlers wore essentially the same style of clothing with the length of the

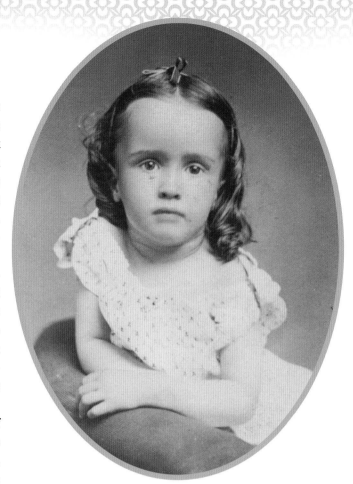

JANE SCHWERDTFEGER

Tell male and female children apart by their hair-styles. The center part identifies this child as a girl.

dress shortened so that movement was permitted. In photographs where boys and girls are dressed alike, one way to tell them apart is by hairstyle. Girls usually wore their hair parted in the middle, while boys' was parted on the side. Since children's clothing styles changed as they grew older, it is possible to estimate the age of children based on their clothing. The length of a girl's skirt was relative to her age—a girl's skirt became gradually longer as she approached adulthood. Boys wore short pants until they were teenagers.

When you examine your photographs for costume details, you may notice that clothing was used to convey a sense of belonging to a group. Sports teams and club group portraits often feature members all wearing a certain style of clothing. For instance, theatrical performers in the late nineteenth century often sat for portraits to commemorate a play. Group portraits provide clues to activities in which your ancestors took part. The costume of a team may not only help you date the image, but will add additional information to your family history.

Clothing styles also reflected changes within a family. During pregnancy or while working around the house, women wore loose dresses called wrappers. Graduation photos of young women show them dressed entirely in white—including their shoes. A whole ritual of fashion surrounded mourning. The presence of black crepe on the collars and cuffs of a woman's dress indicates she is in mourning. Social conventions merged with fashion so that the prevalence of black accessories could suggest the length of time a woman was in mourning. Recent widows wore all black, while those in extended mourning could wear white accessories.

Immigrants often abandoned full ethnic dress upon arrival to America in order to look less like newcomers. However, they might have retained small details to remind them of their homeland—certain accessories can be clues to ethnic identities, such as Spanish mantillas (headscarves) on women or work caps on men.

The best guide to fashion in photographs is Joan L. Severa's *Dressed for the Photographer: Ordinary Americans and Fashion, 1840–1900* (Kent, Ohio: Kent State University Press, 1995). You can learn more about hats and hairstyles in my books, *Fashionable Folks: Hairstyles 1840-1900* and *Fashionable Folks: Bonnets and Hats 1840-1900*. Both are available from Picture Perfect Press.

These charts are based on the images presented in Severa's book and on lectures presented by Nancy Rexford, a leading costume historian. They can be used for comparing styles of clothing. Additional examples appear in the case studies at the end of each chapter.

Women's Fashions

1840–1847

Bodice	Long and tight with fan-shaped gathering; pointed in the front; back fastening.
Neckline	Wide, shallow, horizontal neckline; gradually gets narrower.
Sleeves	Long, tight to arm, with tight oversleeve on upper arms.
Accessories	Fingerless gloves; gold watches on a long chain; caps or bonnets; ribbon bracelets.
Hair	Large combs; center part; close to head; long ringlets.

1848–1852

Bodice	Long and tight with fan shape; pointed in the front; could be padded; back fastening.
Neckline	High collar.
Sleeves	Three-quarter or long, flaring out toward bottom in bell shape, worn over white undersleeve.
Accessories	Fingerless gloves; gold watches on a long chain; caps or bonnets; ribbon bracelets.
Hair	Large combs; center part; close to head; spreading over ears.

COLLECTION OF THE AUTHOR

This is an unidentified woman from the 1840s. Her hair and clothing help date the photo:

1. *Hair looped over her ears with a bun in the back*

2. *Bodice with fan pleats and tight fitting sleeves*

3. *Small cuffs and collars accessorized the outfit*

LIBRARY OF CONGRESS

This group family portrait was taken in 1844.

1. *Emlen Cresson (1811–1889) wears a light-colored shawl-collared vest and dark jacket and tie. His father, Caleb, was a prominent merchant and philanthropist in Philadelphia.*

2. *Cresson's mother, Sarah Emlen Cresson; her attire reflects her Quaker faith—simple dress and cap.*

3. *His wife, Priscilla Prichett Cresson (d. 1902), wears youthful long curls, a striped silk dress and a fur-trimmed wrap.*

4. *Cresson's mother-in-law, Mrs. Edith Hatten Prichett, wears a day-cap and a plain dress adorned with a wide collar and a cloth shawl.*

The date on this daguerreotype is interesting. The Cresson's only child, William, was born in 1843, yet he doesn't appear in this image. William was a promising artist who died at 25 in 1868.

1853–1859

Bodice	Front fastening (near middle of decade); some buttons; some jacket-style, flare overskirt
Neckline	Broad collar; narrower collars at end of period
Sleeves	Flowing wide at the wrists, worn over white undersleeve; some full sleeves gathered into wristband in less formal dresses
Skirt	Wider; full, gathered, or pleated; some flounces; skirt worn over a hoop by end of the decade
Accessories	Decoration of dress; ornamental hair jewelry
Hair	Center part; wide above the ears; then droops over ears

Unidentified man and woman. Francis Grice, photographer, ca. 1855.

1. In the 1850s, women wore their hair with extreme puffs on the side of the head. Hairstyles like this were often padded with false hair or hair saved from hair brushes.

2. She wears a scalloped collar and white undersleeves peek from her wide bell sleeves.

3. He wears a plaid vest and his arm rests protectively on the back of her chair.

Both the style of this case and of the woman's bonnet establish the date of this unidentified portrait as c. 1855.

1860–1865

Bodice	Front buttons; pointed or round waists, military trim
Neckline	High, narrow round collar; some V-necks with lapels
Sleeves	Armhole over shoulder; some gathered into the wrist; some wide bell; some coat sleeves wider at elbow; variety of styles
Skirt	Full, pleated, some looped up to expose underskirt; worn over hoop
Accessories	Shawls, hair nets, wide belts; elaborate earrings and brooches
Hair	Center part; covers most of ear, plain or braids around; short ringlets

1866–1868

Bodice	Front buttons; short waist; slightly raised waistline
Neckline	High, with narrow round or pointed collar; lace or ribbon tie
Sleeves	Armhole over shoulder; narrower coat sleeve
Skirt	Broad A-line shape over hoop, few pleats in front
Accessories	Shawls
Hair	Center part; pulled tightly back above the ears, piled high in back

COLLECTION OF THE AUTHOR

This unidentified couple was photographed c. 1865.

1. *The Soutache braid on her dress helps place this image in the late 1860s.*

2. *Notice her small round collar, belted waist and sleeves gathered at the wrist.*

3. *Her hair is behind her ears in a net.*

4. *Drop earrings accessorize her dress.*

5. *He wears a long frock style coat with thin bow tie.*

1869-1874

Bodice	Trim such as ruffles; prominent buttons large, not flat
Neckline	High with low stand collar or V-neck with ruffles
Sleeves	Armhole over shoulder; wider coat sleeves with cuff effects; moderate bell with trim or ruffles
Skirt	Trimmed apron-like overskirt with bustle over trimmed underskirt; large bustle
Accessories	Black velvet neck ribbon with brooch or charm; large lockets and crosses; jet beads; earrings and necklace matched
Hair	Center part; use of false hair; large hair combs; some hair curled at forehead; long hair streaming down back with hair braided at crown

1875-1877

Bodice	Often ruffles around neckline and down front
Neckline	Front opening, low stand collar or V-neck with ruffles
Sleeves	Sleeves narrower, still cuff trim
Skirt	Long overskirt effects, bustle less large; trains common
Accessories	Large button earrings; large hair combs
Hair	Center part; frizzed at forehead; braided high at back

This is a photo of a well-dressed woman of the 1870s. In the 1870s, women wore large looped hair. In this case, it's a hair piece. Notice the difference between the quality of the curls and her natural hair. High collars and large jewelry (earrings and necklaces) were fashionable in this decade.

Unidentified couple, 1876–1878

1. This woman wears the fashionable fringed cuirass form fitting bodice that extends past her hips.

2. Her overskirt features horizontal pleats, bows, fringe and a ruffle.

3. Around her neck she wears a scarf.

4. While many women in the 1870s wore full hairstyles, she chose to pull her hair back.

5. Her companion wears a long frock coat, which was usually reserved for formal occasions in the 1870s.

6. He wears his hair combed back.

Women's Fashions

1878–1882

Bodice	Front buttons; flat and large round or oval buttons; bodice extends over hips
Neckline	High with low stand collar
Sleeves	Sleeves narrower
Skirt	Fell straight from hip to floor
Accessories	Fans, parasols
Hair	Center part; frizzing, low at back

1883–1889

Bodice	Tight, waistcoat effects; bodice extends just below the waist
Neckline	High with low stand collar, fewer lace ties
Sleeves	Sleeves tight, three-quarter length, trim at bottom
Skirt	Draped overskirt, often apron-like in shape
Accessories	Muffs, jewelry
Hair	Frizzed around forehead; bun in back

This is a photo of two friends taken in the late 1880s.

1. Tall hats with lots of trim were very fashionable in this decade.

2. Watch for large buttons and form fitting bodices.

3. Large bustles were common.

This unidentified couple was photographed c. 1890.

1. Peaked shoulder seams are a sign of the circa 1890 period.

2. Her bodice is fitted with a wide lace collar found in the 1880s.

3. Her skirt has horizontal pleats and a scalloped hem.

4. His very full beard is typical of the 1880s.

5. Tucking the tie under the collar is also typical of the 1880s.

1890–1892

Bodice	Fastening obscured; ends at or near natural waist
Neckline	High neck with moderate stand collar
Sleeves	Tight to arm in 1890, with kick-up at shoulder becoming fuller each year
Skirt	Drapery gradually smoothes out to stiff columnar shape
Accessories	Round brooch; small earrings; watch pinned to bosom; large fans; large parasols
Hair	Frizzed around face; bun on top of head

1893–1896

Bodice	Fastening obscured; ruffles over shoulders; gathers in bodice
Neckline	High collar to chin with bow at side back
Sleeves	Ruffles, large balloon "leg-of-mutton" shapes on upper arm; tight below
Skirt	Smooth at hips; front/sides; gradual flare to stiff A-line effect; sometimes trim at the hem
Accessories	Feather boa; large fans; parasols
Hair	Frizzed; curled around face; bun in back

1897–1900

Bodice	Asymmetrical, horizontal drapery; blouse-like fullness overhangs waist at center front
Neckline	High collar to chin, bow at side back of neck
Sleeves	Decreasing, first small ball-shaped fullness at top, then tight, flaring over hand
Skirt	Smooth at hip front/sides; broad A-line becomes slimmer, may flare out below knees
Accessories	Round brooch; small earrings; watch pinned to bosom; small decorative combs high on back of head visible from front
Hair	Soft but smoother around face, less frizzing; drawn into back bun

This unidentified couple was photographed, c. 1898.

1. *Large top-knots were all the rage at the end of the nineteenth century.*

2. *Leg-of-mutton style sleeves—tight on the lower arm and puffed at the shoulder—were also very popular.*

3. *His mustache is waxed in the style of the late 1890s.*

4. *Men often wore upturned collars with bow ties.*

Unidentified woman, c.1910.

1901–1903

Bodice	Pouched front pronounced
Neckline	High collar to chin
Sleeves	Fullness increasing year by year on lower arm above cuff only
Skirt	Smooth at hip front/sides; flares from knee down
Hair	Soft but smoother around face, less frizzing; drawn into back bun

1904–1907

Bodice	Pouched front continues over wider waistbands
Neckline	High collar to chin; a few collarbone-level in summer
Sleeves	1904: fullness on upper and lower arms; 1905–07: fullness only on upper, sleeves appear to be made in upper and lower sections
Skirt	Smooth at hips or soft gathers or pleats; generally less slim
Hair	Gradually gaining width around the face; coiled in back

1908–1914

Bodice	Vertical trim effects, small square or round dickey effects; waistline often slightly raised
Neckline	High collar to chin or round/square to collarbone
Sleeves	Increasingly tight and plain; some imitate tight lace undersleeves
Skirt	Increasingly slim, straight, no gathers, feet show
Hair	Some center parts; puffed out wide at sides to support big hats

A girl and her teacher, c. 1910.

1. *Watch for captions. Without this label it would be easy to think this image depicts a mother and daughter.*

2. *Little girls often wore bows in their hair in the early twentieth century.*

3. *Women in the first decade of the century wore their hair full with a bun on the top.*

4. *As more women entered the workplace, fashion became functional, such as this woman's blouse and skirt ensemble.*

A group of friends or family out for a summer outing, c.1910.

1. *Women wore corsets to make their waists as small as possible.*

2. *Men's removable shirt collars were high and starched.*

3. *Women's hats were oversized with large feathers.*

4. *No well-dressed woman would go outside without a parasol to shield her from the sun.*

5. *There were a large variety of ties in the early twentieth century. These men chose thin ones.*

1840–1850

Coats	Extra-long, narrow sleeves
Shirt	Dress: tailored white cotton; narrow sleeves; small collar turned up under a tie Work: colors and patterns or smocks
Necktie	Tied in a horizontal bowknot, dark colored
Trousers	Fly-front
Hair & Beard	Ear-length, parted high at one side; clean shaven but fringe beards

1850–1860

Coats	Generous cut; vests
Shirt	Collar turned over the tie Dress: pleated starched bib fronts Work: colors and patterns Shirt fronts could be purchased
Necktie	2" wide half-bow
Trousers	Fly-front; wide pant legs
Hair & Beard	Clean-shaven; end of decade full beards appear; oiled hair, long on top, combed into wave at center of forehead; collar length; side part; ears covered later in the decade

1860–1870

Coats	Long, overlarge sack coats
Shirt	Collars folded down around the neck; white, stripes, and plaids
Necktie	Narrow
Trousers	Wide, longer at the heel; suspenders common
Hair & Beard	Chin whiskers; hair at ear level in back; side part

1870–1880

Coats	Shorter and closefitting; narrower; buttoned at top button only to show vest
Shirt	Made without collars; collars purchased; white, blue, red, black, or gray stripes, small plaids
Necktie	Wide and tied in a loose knot; ends overlap; striped
Accessories	Fur hats and coats

1880–1890

Coats	Short sacks; narrow sleeves high on shoulder
Shirt	White
Necktie	Variety of ties, wide and soft
Trousers	Narrow with no creases

COLLECTION OF THE AUTHOR

The back of this photo of an unidentified young man is dated 1880. Short, tight fitting jackets epitomized the decade. Men wore their hair short and their ties under shirt collars.

Men in work clothes

1. A "dandy"—a well dressed man in the current style of the early twentieth century

2. A laborer

3. A conservative office worker

1890–1900

Coats	Narrow, small coats buttoned all the way to the top
Shirt	Trim-fitted white shirts; small, stiff collars; collar may be very high and stiff by 1900
Necktie	Black bow tie; narrow ties of black or patterns
Trousers	Narrow
Hair & Beard	Short haircuts; large mustaches

RESOURCES FOR COSTUME DATING

Web Sites

ACCESSIBLE ARCHIVES, INC.
<www.accessible.com>
Subscription archive of eighteenth- and nineteenth-century publications, including *Godey's Lady's Book* 1830–1880.

COSTUME SOCIETY OF AMERICA
<www.costumesocietyamerica.com>
Learn more about costume from this professional organization of costume historians.

INTERNATIONAL COSTUMER'S GUILD, INC.
<www.costume.org>
The mission of the International Costumers' Guild is to "bring hobbyist and professional costumers from around the world together, and to foster, through its chapters, local educational, and social costume events."

SAUNDRA ROS ALTMAN'S PAST PATTERNS
<www.pastpatterns.com>
Historically accurate nineteenth- and early twentieth-century clothing patterns for men, women, and children.

Books

Costume of Household Servants, From the Middle Ages to 1900 by Phillis Cunnington (New York: Barnes & Noble Books, 1975).

Dress in American Culture edited by Patricia A. Cunningham and Susan Voso Lab (Bowling Green, Ohio: Bowling Green State University Popular Press, 1993).

Dressed for the Job: The Story of Occupational Costume by Christobel Williams-Mitchell (New York: Blandford, 1982).

Dressed for the Photographer: Ordinary Americans and Fashion, 1840-1900 by Joan L. Severa (Kent, Ohio: Kent State University Press, 1995).

Everyday Fashions 1909-1920 as Pictured in Sears Catalogs edited by JoAnne Olian (New York: Dover Publications, 1995).

Everyday Fashions of the Forties as Pictured in Sears Catalogs edited by JoAnne Olian (New York: Dover Publications, 1992).

Everyday Fashions of the Thirties as Pictured in Sears Catalogs edited by Stella Blum (New York: Dover Publications, 1986).

Everyday Fashions of the Twenties as Pictured in Sears and Other Catalogs edited by Stella Blum (New York: Dover Publications, 1981).

Fashions in Hair: The First Five Thousand Years by Richard Corson (New York: Hillary House, 1969).

MAGAZINES AND CATALOGS DATING COSTUME AND INTERIORS

American Girl 1920–1979
Brides 1934–present
Cosmopolitan 1886–present
Designer and the Woman's Magazine 1894–1926
Essence 1970–present
Frank Leslie's Lady's Journal 1871–1881
Glamour 1939–present
Godey's Lady's Book 1830–1898
Good Housekeeping 1885–present
Harper's Bazaar 1867–present
Ladies Home Journal 1883–present
Mademoiselle 1935–present
McCall's 1876–present
Modern Bride 1949–present
Peterson Magazine 1842–1898
Redbook 1903–present
Seventeen 1944–present
Simplicity Fashion Magazine 1963
Vogue 1890–present
Woman's Day 1937–present
Woman's Home Companion 1873–1957
Women's Wear Daily 1910–present
Working Woman 1976–present
Young Miss (YM) 1955–present

STORE CATALOGS

Jordan Marsh
Marshall Field
Montgomery Ward
Sears, Roebuck and Co.

An Illustrated History of Hairstyles 1830-1930 by Marian I. Doyle (Atglen, Pa.: Schiffer Publications, 2003).

Mirror, Mirror: A Social History of Fashion by Michael and Ariane Batterberry (New York: Holt, Rinehart and Winston, 1977).

Mourning Dress: A Costume and Social History by Lou Taylor (Boston: G. Allen and Unwin, 1983).

20th Century Fashion: The Complete Sourcebook by John Peacock (London: Thames & Hudson, 1993).

Victorian Fashions and Costumes from Harper's Bazaar, 1867–1898 edited by Stella Blum (New York: Dover Publications, 2012).

With Grace & Favor: Victorian & Edwardian Fashion in America by Otto Charles Thieme et al. (Cincinnati, Ohio: Cincinnati Art Museum, 1993).

Men

Civil War Gentlemen: 1860s Apparel Arts & Uniforms by R.L. Shep and W.S. Salisbury (Mendocino, Calif.: R.L. Shep, 1994).

Men's Fashion: The Complete Sourcebook by John Peacock (London: Thames & Hudson, 1996).

Finding the Civil War in Your Family Album by Maureen Taylor (Westwood, Ma : Picture Perfect Press, 2011).

Women

Dress and Undress: A History of Women's Underwear by Elizabeth Ewing (New York: Drama Book Specialists, 1978).

Historic Dress in America, 1607–1870 by Elisabeth McClellan (New York: Tudor Publishing Co., 1989).

Victorian Costume for Ladies, 1860–1900 by Linda Setnik (Atglen, Pa: Schiffer Publications, 2000).

What We Wore: An Offbeat Social History of Women's Clothing, 1950–1980 by Ellen Melinkoff (New York: W. Morrow, 1984).

Children

Children's Clothes Since 1750 by Clare Rose (London: B.T. Batsford, 1989).

The Child in Fashion, 1750 to 1920 by Kristina Harris (Atglen, Pa.: Schiffer Publications, 1999).

COLLECTION OF THE AUTHOR

The fashionably dressed young woman in this photograph has been identified by her descendants as Alice McDuff. My family knew the image was once in Alice's possession and wanted to find out when the photograph was taken and for what purpose. It is possible that this photograph was taken around the time of her wedding in 1916.

The imprint on this cabinet card identifies the photographer as Harbeck of Pawtucket, Rhode Island. City directory research for Harbeck lists a Jean L. Harbeck of Pawtucket in the photographic business from 1903 to 1940. This does not assign a more specific date to the image.

Upon close examination of the image, the key elements of the outfit are identified: high waist; fitted bodice and skirt; lots of trim and buttons, high neckline, and ankle-length skirt. By consulting John Peacock's *20th Century Fashion: The Complete Sourcebook* (London: Thames & Hudson, 1993) and comparing the photo to his sketches, a tentative date for the photograph based on costume is 1910–1916.

The accessories help assign a final date. Alice is wearing a watch pinned to the bodice of her dress and a locket around her neck. A family member owns both pieces of jewelry, but neither one has a date engraved on it. The locket is a friendship token with Alice and a friend's initials engraved on the exterior of the piece. The watch is identified as a Molly Stark model manufactured by the Hampden Watch Company of Canton, Ohio. Alice is also wearing this watch in an earlier family group portrait.

The final key to the mystery can be found in the ring on her left hand. The photographer posed her so that the ring is a prominent feature of the portrait. It is almost certain that this photograph and one of her husband taken at the same time are a pair of wedding portraits. Alice McDuff and Joseph Bessette were married in 1916. The costume clues and genealogical data support this conclusion.

Accessories

Bags and Purses by Vanda Foster (London: B.T. Batsford, 1982).

A Certain Style: The Art of the Plastic Handbag, 1949–59 edited by Robert Gottlieb and Frank Maresca (New York: Alfred A. Knopf, 1988).

Fashionable Folks: Hairstyles 1840-1900 by Maureen Taylor (Westwood, MA: Picture Perfect Press, 2009).

Fashionable Folks: Bonnets and Hats 1840-1900 by Maureen Taylor (Westwood, MA: Picture Perfect Press, 2011).

Gloves by Valerie Cumming (London: B.T. Batsford, 1982).

Hats in Vogue Since 1910 edited by Christina Probert (New York: Abbeville Press, 1981).

Heavenly Soles: Extraordinary Twentieth-Century Shoes by Mary Trasko (New York: Abbeville Press, 1989).

Jewelry in America, 1600–1900 by Martha Gandy Fales (Woodbridge, Suffolk, U.K.: Antique Collectors' Club, 1995).

Shawls, Crinolines, Filigree: The Dress and Adornment of the Women of New Mexico, 1739–1900 by Carmen Espinosa. (El Paso, Tex.: Texas Western Press, 1970).

Shoes by June Swan (London: B.T. Batsford, 1982).

20th Century Jewelry: The Complete Sourcebook by John Peacock (New York: Thames & Hudson, 2002).

Vintage Hats & Bonnets, 1770–1970: Identification & Values by Susan Langley (Paducah, Ky.: Collector Books, 1998).

You see, but you do not observe..."

—Sir Arthur Conan Doyle, "A Scandal In Bohemia," *The Adventures of Sherlock Holmes*, 1890

10

Reading the Clues in Photographs

Three specific types of images in your family photograph collection deserve extra attention. The complexities of wedding pictures, military images, and those taken in foreign lands require another dimension to your photo research. While it's usually easy to recognize a photograph of someone in uniform, identifying a wedding picture can be difficult, and the same can be true of immigrant images unless the person depicted is wearing ethnic dress. Answering the where, when, how, and what of these three types of pictures can be challenging, but rewarding. Here's how to read the clues in your family album.

1860s
Marriage portraits taken in the actual outfits the bride and groom wore during the wedding ceremony gain popularity.

1870s–1880s
Fashion-conscious brides select colors for their wedding dresses from the new synthetic dyes, such as brown.

1880s
Wedding albums become popular.

1863–present
Badges or insignia pins worn on military headgear identify the corps with whom a solider serves.

1872–1904
Plumed and spiked military helmets are part of dress occasions.

1892–1924
More than 20 million people immigrate to America through Ellis Island.

MATRIMONIAL IMAGES

As you look through your family photographs, it may seem unusual that there aren't as many pictures of bridal parties as there are of marriages. After all, today's brides not only hire professional photographers to compile formal albums, but even ask guests to take pictures of each other with single-use cameras on every table. Also, the stereotypical photograph of a bride and groom doesn't always exist for weddings in the nineteenth and early twentieth century because the style, the importance, and even the look of wedding photographs were different. Humorous photographs offered for sale at the turn of the twentieth century depicted each step in a young couple's courtship and marriage, from engagement to honeymoon. While many of those stages haven't changed today, their photographic documentation has. You may have wedding pictures in your family collection and not recognize them for what they are. So take another look at all your photographs of couples and single portraits of young men and women. A photograph might hold the answer to one of your genealogical challenges, such as the date and place of your great grandparents' wedding: You know—the one that isn't recorded anywhere. Photographs can help you uncover your family's romantic past if you know what to look for.

Wedding portraits can establish the marriage dates of ancestors, c.1905.

Photo Identification Tips

So how can you find those wedding images in your family album? Start with your family tree. Make a list of all marriages since the advent of photography in 1839 and include when and where they occurred. Try to match up those names with photographs in your collection. The same identification techniques used to date a picture will help you discover your family's visual wedding history. Be sure to see if there's a caption on the back that identifies it as a wedding image, possibly a date you already know one of your ancestors was married on. If the picture remains unidentified, try the following tips:

- Look at those unknown images and see if any clues are visible, such as photographic method or the name of the photographer.

- Take copies of unidentified images with you whenever you visit relatives—you never know when Uncle George or Cousin Sarah may recognize the faces in the pictures or have a few wedding photographs from their collection to share. They may even have a story or two about family weddings they've attended, so keep a tape recorder handy to record them.

- If you haven't already done so, find actual documents that record family weddings, such as marriage intentions, licenses, and church records. The names of the witnesses may help you identify members of the wedding party in a group portrait. A photograph becomes more important to family history when you have names, stories, and documents to go with it.

- Clothing can be a very accurate way to identify a marriage portrait—so it helps to know something about the history of wedding costume and traditions. For example, the identification may ultimately be revealed by a tiny, obscure detail only common to weddings of the 1870s.

Clothing Clues

"Here comes the bride, all dressed in white." This may be the beginning of a traditional wedding song, but that modern image is not always accurate for the past. Purchasing a white dress to be worn just once was expensive, and many individuals chose to wear their best outfit instead. Frugal Victorian brides who wore white often altered their wedding dresses for special occasions, so look for that dress in other images as well. Brides actually wore a variety of attire, including the familiar white gown but certainly not limited to it. Dresses reflect the fashions of the era in which the couple married. Colors for wedding dresses varied from blue, signifying fidelity, to purple, a memorial to the Civil War dead. In the 1870s and 1880s, fashion-conscious brides selected dress colors from the new synthetic dyes like brown. That's one reason the woman in the photo on the right posed so proudly in her brown-corded silk dress on her wedding day. She was making a fashion statement.

Dating an image based on clothing can place an image within a couple of years. However, be careful when estimating dates for wedding dresses—there is a long-standing tradition of wearing your mother or grandmother's dress. In one photograph I've seen, the groom wore clothing from the 1930s but the bride's dress dated from the late nineteenth century. She updated her look with a new veil. It is necessary to look at each piece of a bride's outfit to make sure that the dress and the accessories are from the same time period.

Certain accessories are associated with brides, regardless of their dress selection. Veils, flowers, and bows decorated even the plainest marriage attire, and consequently can identify a wedding portrait. Orange blossoms, the choice of Queen Victoria when she married Prince Albert, remained an important decoration for decades. Even men wore small sprigs of blossoms attached to their coats to signify a wedding. According to an etiquette book from 1901, affluent young women could wear their first tiara at their wedding. Economical brides might borrow a veil, since wearing something

Not all brides wore white, so examine your family portraits carefully for other evidence of a marriage, 1876.

borrowed is a tradition. Or the veil may be a family heirloom paired with a new dress.

Consult fashion books such as Joan L. Severa's *Dressed for the Photographer: Ordinary American's and Fashion, 1840–1900* to compare your wedding photographs to other images from the same time. You can also find examples of well-dressed bridal parties in American women's magazines, such as *Godey's Lady's Book* (1830–1898) and *Brides* (1934–present).

Portraits and Albums

Photography may date back to 1839, but that doesn't mean there are wedding images that early in your family. According to Barbara Norfleet, author of *Wedding* (New York: Simon and Schuster, 1979), not many people posed for formal wedding pictures during the first thirty years of photography. Couples sat for portraits before or after the wedding, but not in their formal attire. Of course, some did, and those images are valuable and sought after by collectors.

By the late 1860s, more couples had portraits taken in their wedding clothes or paid a photographer to come to their home to photograph them. Some women gave away those photographs of themselves to their family and friends as mementos of the event. One woman signed the back of her wedding portrait, "With much love to my own dear Beatie, Souvenir of Jan. 14th, 1896."

Wedding albums had become popular by the 1880s. Rather than just focusing on the couple, photographers began including members of the wedding party. Victorian couples received gifts prior to the wedding and laid them out for guests to view. You can find pictures of these lavish displays in Victorian albums. These images are a visual document of what affluent couples received when they married. By closely examining them, you might discover artifacts still in the family.

Poses

When you look at a portrait taken in a studio, initially you may not notice how the photographer arranged the subjects. Photographers choreographed the portrait both to capture the couple's personality and to demonstrate their own skill. After all, couples showing off their wedding images attracted business for the photographer.

- Is the man standing or sitting? Photographers generally posed men standing. If the opposite is true, it might mean that the man is extremely tall or the pose may indicate something about the couple's relationship.

- Is the couple standing close together? While some couples are obviously self-conscious in front of a camera, others show their love by leaning toward each other or holding hands. The attraction visible in these images is worthy of any contemporary romantic fiction.

- In a group portrait of family with the couple, can you tell who is on the groom's side and who is on the bride's? In family portraits, the relatives usually stay to the side of the person to whom they are related.

- The bridal pose also suggests a date for the image. Bridal portraits with the woman looking directly into the camera were popular in the nineteenth century, but were replaced by those with brides looking away in the twentieth century.

Ethnic and Religious Evidence

Wedding pictures can also provide clues to your family's origins. The colors and style of a bridal dress and her choice of accessories may signify ethnic origins. Even the setting of the wedding can reveal immigrant roots. Adding a culturally significant headdress to an outfit is one way that new immigrants combined American and Old World wedding traditions. You might have pictures of weddings that occurred in the country of origin. Architectural details can sometimes suggest if a photograph was not taken in America. Robert Harrold's *Folk Costumes of the World* (London: Cassell, 1999) has examples of native clothing that can assist with identification.

COLLECTION OF THE AUTHOR

The broom in this tintype suggests it is a wedding portrait, 1880s.

BOOKS FOR WEDDING PORTRAIT IDENTIFICATION

A Bride's Book of Wedding Traditions by Arlene Hamilton Stewart (New York: Hearst Books, 1995).

To Love and to Cherish: Brides Remembered by Linda Otto Lipsett (Lincolnwood, Ill.: Quilt Digest Press, 1997).

You Are Cordially Invited to Weddings: Dating & Love Customs of Cultures Worldwide, Including Royalty by Carolyn Mordecai (Phoenix, Ariz.: Nittany Publishing, 1999).

Wedded Bliss: A Victorian Bride's Handbook by Molly Dolan Blayney (New York: Abbeville Press, 1992).

Wedding Fashions, 1862–1912: 380 Costume Designs from "La Mode Illustree" edited by JoAnne Olian (New York: Dover Publications, 1994).

COLLECTION OF THE AUTHOR

My grandfather wore a good quality suit for his wedding, 1916.

Pictures of a bride and groom might also contain symbols that reflect religious customs. For instance, brooms are part of some African-American ceremonies and huppas (special canopies) indicate a Jewish wedding. If you don't know your ancestor's religion, a wedding portrait can provide the key.

Family History and the Wedding Portrait

Don't limit your wedding search to images of the couple on their wedding day. Create a story of the couple with their marriage certificate, invitations, photographs, the minister who performed the ceremony, and the place where they were married. In the nineteenth century, preprinted forms could be purchased that held small photographs of the bride, groom, and in some cases, the minister, along with the date and place of the wedding. These were suitable for framing and hung in many homes. There may also be artifacts in your family that add to the tale, such as linens or wedding gowns. In some families, quilts are part of the wedding tradition.

Never stop looking for pictures to tell the visual history of the people on your family tree. Just because an image doesn't appear to be a wedding portrait, don't discount it until you've had time to establish a date for the image and compare that time frame to known wedding dates for that person.

If you can't find a wedding picture of your ancestors, there is always the possibility that one doesn't exist. For example, not everyone could afford to have a portrait taken in the mid-nineteenth century. In some families, the lack of wedding pictures may indicate a conflict over the marriage, such as parental disapproval or an elopement. Once you have a wedding portrait—or even if you don't—try to find a picture of the church or even the minister to fill in your family's photographic heritage.

MILITARY IMAGES

Every photograph tells a story, but this is especially true for images of a man or woman in uniform. All you have to do to uncover the tale is know how to read the message in the picture. Of additional help are the oral history tales generally passed on from generation to generation about your ancestor's participation in military conflicts like the Civil War.

Basic photo identification techniques involve determining the style of photograph, looking at the costume clues, dating when a photographer was in business, and paying attention to details. All photographic detective work takes an observant eye, a magnifying glass, and—like many genealogical pursuits—a little patience. This is particularly true when examining a photograph of someone in uniform. Deciphering the details in a portrait depicting military service usually involves additional research, connecting with experts, and tracking down supplementary evidence. The good news is that you can learn a lot from military photos regardless of whether you know who's in the picture.

Start With Family

Search your family photograph collection for pictures of people in uniform and ask your relatives to do the same. While there were individuals in the armed services between major conflicts, most men either volunteered or were drafted to participate in the significant wars in American history, including the American Revolution (1775–1783), the War of 1812 (1812–1815), the Mexican War (1846–1848), the Civil War (1861–1865), the Spanish-American War (1898), World War I (1917–1918), World War II (1941–1945), and modern military conflicts such as Korea, Vietnam, and the current campaign in Iraq. Even though the American Revolution and the War of 1812 pre-date the advent of photography in 1839, you still might have images of veterans of these wars mixed in with your photographs.

Don't immediately exclude the photographs of women in your family from your military research. Women historically supported war efforts through a variety of activities, such as volunteering for various groups and serving as nurses. You might have photo albums recording your great-grandmother's exploits during World War I when she served doughnuts to soldiers while with the Red Cross.

COLLECTION OF THE AUTHOR

Military photographs can help you find other service records.

Learn the History

Establishing a time frame for an unidentified photograph is especially important for a portrait of someone in uniform. Besides dating when they served, you'll also want to determine the branch of the service. Scrutinize the images for clues and research the background history of the armed forces. Various uniform changes through the years can make dating a photograph of someone in uniform a challenge. Besides visiting the public library, you can also contact one of the regional chapters of the Company of Military Historians **<www. military-historians.org>**. This educational, literary, and scientific organization consists of researchers, historians, and collectors that study all aspects of military history in the United States and the Western Hemisphere. They publish a quarterly journal, T*he Military Collector & Historian.*

Clothing

Clothing clues present in a portrait can be especially revealing when the person depicted wears a uniform. There are variations in military dress throughout history in all parts of the world. Trying to decipher the subtle changes in uniform style is an acquired skill. Being able to see the differences in dress and symbol can lead you to new discoveries about an ancestor. There are a number of unique things to look for that can immediately solve a mystery. During the Civil War, many Union volunteers wore belt buckles with a state abbreviation signifying their state of enlistment, while Confederate soldiers often wore buckles with "CSA" engraved on them, for Confederate States of America. The details in those Union belt buckles suggest a place to start looking for documentary evidence of military service. You might have been looking in the wrong state. My own ancestors lived in Rhode Island, but enlisted in a nearby Massachusetts town. A photograph of one of them in uniform wearing an initialed belt buckle would have saved me hours of pointless research.

Here are some other costume details to look for.

HEADGEAR

During the Civil War (1861–1865), long crowned kepis or hats dominated the uniform. However, by the mid-1880s, the hat shape became small and tilted because of changes in military regulations. Plumed, spiked helmets were part of dress occasions from 1872 to 1904. During this period, German military methods and dress were admired, so these spiked helmets became part of American military dress. Two collectors of these helmets, Mark Kasal and Don Moore, wrote *A Guide Book to U.S. Army Dress Helmets, 1872–1904* (Tustin, Calif.: North Cape Publications, 2000) that is invaluable if you have a portrait of a man wearing one of these helmets. In World War I, soldiers were issued an "overseas cap" once they arrived. Start deciphering the costume clues by breaking the uniform down into pieces and establishing a date for each based on its unique characteristics.

SHIRTS AND PANTS

It can be difficult to tell the difference between uniforms used in the Civil War and those worn post-war because of re-use. Compare your pictures to images in the books listed in the resource section and then add up all your clues—type of image, photographers' dates, and family information—to make sure they agree.

DECORATION

Cloth chevrons on the sleeves and shoulders of a uniform and insignia on the collar or headgear signified rank. Starting in 1863, badges or insignia pins worn on the headgear identified the corps the soldier served with. In the Navy, hashmarks (cloth stripes) on the sleeves stand for the number of years of service. A portrait of someone in full-dress uniform would include medals, braids, ribbons, and even sashes, depending on the time period.

WEAPONS AND EQUIPMENT

If the soldier posed with his full gear, look carefully at the type of sword or firearm he carried and don't forget his everyday equipment, including a canteen. Each one is an important detail. A man carrying a carbine is probably part of the cavalry, while a man with a pistol could be an officer.

VETERANS

Do you know if any of your ancestors joined a veterans group like the Grand Army of the Republic after the Civil War, or the Veterans of Foreign Wars? Clues that an ancestor belonged to a veteran's group may be a little hard to see without a magnifying glass—it may only be

COLLECTION OF THE AUTHOR

Nineteenth century uniforms featured distinctive headgear.

I found this photo while searching the Library of Congress (LOC) Web site **<www.loc.gov>** for a Civil War period photo. The LOC cataloging record for the image (found on the "About this Image" tab) suggests it was taken between June 1864 and April 1865. The title of the photo, "City Point, Virginia. Brig. Gen. John A. Rawlins, Chief of Staff with wife and child at door of their quarters," was supplied by the photo's original collectors, Hirst D. Milhollen and Donald H. Mugridge.

I instantly wanted to know the names of the wife and child. I also wanted to know about Rawlins and wondered about the importance of City Point.

Finding more about City Point was easy. It was the Union headquarters of General Ulysses S. Grant during the Siege of Petersburg fought between June 9, 1864 and March 25, 1865.

With a little research, I was able to find answers to my other questions.

I started by researching Rawlins. A quick web search identified John A. Rawlins as Chief of Staff to General Grant, but the Wikipedia citation didn't list his wife or child's name. Another web search for *"John A. Rawlins"* turned up a biography of him on Find A Grave **<findagrave.com>**, a Web site that contains pictures of tombstones and burial information from thousands of cemeteries around the world. This information is supplied

LIBRARY OF CONGRESS

by users of the site. As always, it's a good idea to verify the information found on the Web.

Rawlins had two wives, Emily Smith Rawlins (1833–1861) and Mary Emeline Hurlburt Rawlins (1840–1874). So which wife was in this photo? The bio contained a link for Mary Emeline Hurlburt Rawlins, and clicking through it led me to a short biography of her as well as a photo,

revealed in the form of a small pin on the jacket lapel. If you own a group portrait of men and women standing in front of Mount Vernon, home of George Washington, it could be a reunion picture for a branch of the Grand Army of the Republic, since many Civil War veterans groups visited there.

FINDING NEW PICTURES

Your family photograph collection might be lacking images of the men and women who served, but that doesn't mean you can't find some. There are many ways to locate family photographs missing from your collection, from networking to looking in the right places. For more information on building a family photograph collection, consult chapter eleven.

Network

Try contacting battle re-enactment groups—many of them collect historical material. A simple search using an Internet search engine like Google can connect you with others interested in the history of a particular regiment, or even living veterans of twentieth-century conflicts. Another option is to track down descendants of people who served in the same regiment as your family member. This can be especially fruitful for World War I, World War II, Korea, and Vietnam.

Search Libraries

Military service photos include portraits of individuals in uniform, regimental group portraits, war scenes, and photo albums of wartime activities. These pictures

which I compare to this photo. The facial features (eyes, nose, mouth and facial shape) matched, confirming that the woman in the photo is Mary.

Rawlins met Mary in Vicksburg, Mississippi, during the famous siege of the city and, according to Connecticut Marriages 1729–1867 (available at **<familysearch.org>**), he married her on December 22, 1863.

The wife is identified, but who is the child? According to their bios on Find a Grave, John had at least three, possibly four, children with his first wife and at least two, possibly three, with his second. Two of the children John and Mary had together were born after the Civil War, so that eliminates them from consideration. The girl in the photo is one of John's daughters from his first marriage. She is either Jane (b. 1858) or Emily (b. 1860). The girl in this picture is likely between 5 and 10 years old.

When and where was this photo taken? I searched Google Books **<books.google.com>** and found a free digital copy of *The Life of John A. Rawlins* by James Harrison Wilson (Neale Publishing, 1916). Still using Google Books, I did a keyword search for *City Point* in the book. The search brought up a references to a possible visit to City Point made by Mrs. Grant accompanied by Mary Rawlins. The letter containing the reference was dated November 5, 1864. If the photo caption is correct, the photo probably dates closer to March 1865 when Rawlins was made

Brigadier General. The single star on his shoulders confirms the rank.

The little girl is wearing a lightweight dress more suited for early fall or spring than November. Her stepmother, Mary, wears a dress typical for the mid 1860s. It has a small collar and a hoop skirt. She's accessorized her outfit with a small brimmed hat and the little girl wears one that is similar.

This temporary housing has a shingled roof and a brick chimney. A plank sidewalk protects Rawlins from mud in the rainy season and a boot scraper near the chair is for cleaning his boots before entering his modest dwelling.

If you look at the edges of the print, you can see where the light-sensitive collodion has peeled away from the glass negatives.

According to the cataloging record, this image is part of a set of two. A stereograph consists of two nearly identical prints that when viewed through a stereoscope becomes a three-dimensional image. In this case, only one of the negatives was printed to make this image.

The clothing clues, uniform insignia and other information suggest that this photo was taken in the spring of 1865. After the war, Grant appointed Rawlins his Secretary of War, a post he held until he died of tuberculous in September 1869.

might not be in a family collection, but in a library or historical society. The largest collection of military images from the Mexican-American War to the present is at the United States Army Military History Institute, Attn: Special Collections, 22 Ashburn Drive, Carlisle, PA 17013-5008. Search their digital collection on their Web site **<www.ahco.army.mil>** and order copies of any relevant images.

The index to James C. Neagles' *U.S. Military Records: A Guide to Federal and State Sources, Colonial America to the Present* (Salt Lake City: Ancestry, 1994) contains more than a dozen listings for archives that contain photographs either on the state or national level. The records of the Bureau of Naval Aeronautics (RG 72) at the National Archives include pictures of Navy planes,

BOOKS ON MILITARY UNIFORMS

Battledress: The Uniforms of the World's Great Armies 1700 to the Present edited by I.T. Schick (London: Weidenfeld and Nicolson, 1978).

Military Dress of North America, 1665–1970 by Martin Windrow and Gerry Embleton (New York: Charles Scribner, 1973).

Uniforms of the Civil War in Color by Philip Haythornthwaite (New York: Sterling Publishing Co., 1990).

and the American Battle Monuments Commission in Washington, D.C. has photographs of cemetery markers for soldiers buried overseas during World Wars I and II.

An integral part of researching the military service of your ancestors is looking for service records on the local, state, and national level. Even if the records don't include a photograph, a verbal description of the soldier provides visual details, such as an ancestor's hair and eye color. Use the photographic evidence you've accumulated to locate more material or use documents to hunt for pictures.

The combination of military service records, historical records, and photographs brings your ancestor to life. Use what you've accumulated to tell the story of your family's military service in a format you can share with relatives. You'll be able to capture the attention of even the most disinterested family member because you've taken the time to make genealogy exciting.

IMMIGRANT IMAGES

Photographs of your immigrant ancestors can tell you more than just what they looked like—they often contain evidence of an ancestor's origins and migratory paths. Because foreign images show unfamiliar scenes and include words in other languages, they are often ignored or misunderstood. It's time to rediscover them, because a single photograph can unlock your family history.

If you don't have any images of immigrant ancestors in your home collection, try to find photographs when you do your research. Discovering your family roots in the old country helps you reconnect with relatives and possibly unearth new material and additional photographs. One researcher I know found long-lost cousins in the town her family came from, along with new sources for genealogical data, all because of a single photographic postcard. Be patient and observant in your foreign photo research—often the date is in the little details.

Immigrant photographs present certain challenges to researchers, c.1910.

Oral Traditions

As with any family photograph, ask as many relatives as you can to relate what they know about the image or the people depicted. Use the tips given in chapter two to develop its oral history. The most revealing question you may ask is, "How did it end up in your collection?" Museum curators talk about the "provenance" of an object, meaning the history of ownership. As the family curator, you need to find out more about who owned an image in order to interpret the evidence in an immigrant photograph. A chart documenting who has owned the photo can make it clear who left home and who stayed behind—if someone's in the image but there's no evidence of him in the United States, he most likely stayed in the native country.

Type of Photograph

Determining the type of photograph can be very important in identifying a foreign image. In the mid-nineteenth century, with the exception of the tintype, most photographic techniques originated in Europe. While the daguerreotype and ambrotype remained popular in the United States until the early 1860s, by the 1850s, they were replaced by the paper print in England and France.

Researching Foreign Photographers

After investigating the basic questions regarding a particular image, it's time to begin reading the clues—starting with the person who took the picture. Since the majority of photographs are paper prints, look on the front of the cardboard mount, the back of the image, or at the lower right corner for the photographer's imprint.

Most likely, foreign imprints will require some translation. If you're unfamiliar with the language, consult a special dictionary or an online translation service to help you read the imprint. Even if the locality is written in an alphabet you can read, it may still need translating. For instance, *Copenhagen* can appear as *Kjobenhavn* in an imprint.

Rejoice if your picture contains a photographer's name and address. You'll be able to identify a time frame for when it was taken by establishing when the photographer was in business using directories. Many cities and towns outside of the United States maintained city or trade directories. Consult the list of foreign directories online at Cyndi's List <**www.cyndislist.com**> under the heading "City Directories," or browse materials available

for a particular country by using the World GenWeb site <**www.worldgenweb.org**>.

Compiled lists of photographers also exist online, such as the telnet database at the George Eastman House International Museum of Photography and Film <**www.eastmanhouse.org**>. There are also lists for specific localities like the Index of United Kingdom photographers to 1950 <**www.earlyphotographers.org.uk**> or the Web site <**findingphotographers.homestead.com**>. Look for printed lists by consulting *Photographers: A Sourcebook for Historical Research* edited by Peter E. Palmquist (Nevada City, Calif.: Carl Mautz Publishing, 2000), which includes Richard Rudisill's *Directories of Photographers: An Annotated World Bibliography*.

FOREIGN LANDS

The real challenge is finding information on the place where the picture was taken. Political upheavals often changed country boundaries and wars eliminated many small towns. A historical atlas or gazetteer can usually provide you with a few details about the town that you can use later.

Discovering when and where the photographer of an image operated his business can reveal important details about your family. Immigrants usually frequented photographers who lived in their community and came from the same background. City directories provide dates for when a photographer was in business and census documents can fill in personal details. Directories of photographers also exist. You can find a regional directory and research tips in Palmquist's book. For resources available overseas, check out the WorldGenWeb site <**worldgenweb.org**> for a particular country. Also helpful are the guides published by the Church of Jesus Christ of Latter-day Saints for conducting country-specific research, available online at <**familysearch.org**>.

Another online option is to use search engines. You might get lucky and come across information about a photographer on a family Web page or in a history of photography. Follow the steps for researching photographers outlined in chapter six.

Clothing Clues

Fashionable clothing styles remain somewhat constant regardless of what country the picture was taken in. Pay particular attention to accessories, such as shoes and jewelry when clothing is not in the "current" style. Clothes in a picture offer another way to identify immigrant origins. Most people in urban areas wore clothes that followed the current fashion, which can make identification of the time period, but not the country, easier. As you study your immigrant photos, look for these distinct clothing types that can provide further clues.

Military Uniforms

A significant clue to the original ancestral homeland is finding a picture of a person in military dress. Pay attention to the prominent features of the uniform—hats, braiding, patches, shape and style of pants and jackets, and any props. Then consult one of the many encyclopedias for military dress. The additional clues in a photographer's imprint can narrow down where and when the picture was taken.

Work or Trade Dress

Working men in most countries wore loose shirts, work pants, and sometimes hats. Some tradesmen wore distinctive clothing that identified their occupation and may help place them in a geographic context. Don't forget to look in the background for equipment and working conditions. You can date and place an image based on mechanical contraptions as well as costume.

Ethnic or Regional Variations

Ethnic and regional dress depended on local culture, not necessarily political boundaries. For instance, although Gypsies traveled across Europe, their style of dress didn't necessarily change when they crossed into other countries. Pay attention to any details in a person's dress that do not reflect contemporary fashion—they could be a clue. A photograph of a Japanese family in traditional dress identifies the country of origin, but if there's one family member in contemporary dress, you can estimate a date for the image. Robert Harrold and Phyllida *Legg's Folk Costumes of the World* is a good resource for ethnic dress.

MAGNIFYING THE DETAILS

Once you've translated the photographer's signature and associated clothes with dates and places, it's time to pull out the magnifying glass and pay attention to the photograph's other elements. A stamp, an outdoor sign, a prop, or other details may reveal an important clue.

Ethnic and regional dress can help identify the wearer's country of origin. This woman's headpiece identifies her as being from Macon, Bresse, France, c.1870.

Postal Clues

When postcards became popular in the late nineteenth century, many individuals chose to have their portraits created as postcards to mail to other relatives. Even before postcards, you could mail images along with a letter. A quick trip to your public library can reveal a great deal of data about an old stamp or postmark. An online search of philatelic societies in your area may be helpful if you have trouble finding what you need in postal history books. Stamps can date a picture and place it in a particular country—how much luckier can you get?

As you research your family in another language, it helps to make a list of reference terms that relate to family history. Include family relationships on that list. It could help you decipher the message without using a translation service.

Props

Never underestimate the value of a prop; it may tell you where a picture was taken. Photographers in different countries included a variety of props just as American

Photo research and identification consists of many levels of analysis. It starts with photographic evidence—the costume, the background, the photographer's mark, and any captions. But it also depends largely on family history, local history, and outside sources.

Jake Jacoby sent me this photo, which I featured in two separate posts on the Photo Detective blog at **<blog. familytreemagazine.com/photodetectiveblog>**.

I began with what Jake knew about the photo. He told me that his grandfather Joseph M. Jacoby is seated on the far right in the front. When I asked why his grandfather would be on a ship, Jake responded that he thought his grandfather was welcoming a group of Jewish immigrants from Germany.

Assign a Time Frame

My first step was to analyze the clothing clues to provide a tentative time frame for the image. The width of the sleeves on the woman's dresses and the birds and feathers in their hats suggest that this photo was taken circa 1896 to 1899. The style of the men's suits corroborate these dates.

Gather Family Information

With a timeframe established, I interviewed Jake about his family history and how this picture fits into that context. He is a thorough genealogical researcher, so he was able to share details about his grandfather's life. Joseph Jacoby was born in Mobile, Alabama, in 1865. He appeared in the 1885 Pensacola, Florida, city directory, working as a clerk at P. Stone. Using the information Jake provided, it was easy to put together a timeline of his grandfather's life during the period of this photograph. Joseph lived and worked in Pensacola and he married Esther Myerson on Jan. 4, 1896.

Despite living in Florida, Joseph maintained his ties with family and friends in Mobile. He actually attended temple there. Approximately sixty miles separate the two cities. Family stories relate how Jake's grandfather traveled between Mobile and Pensacola via wagon.

What Jake really wanted to know about this photo was where it was taken. Was his grandfather in Mobile or Pensacola? Jake thinks the photo was taken in Mobile rather than Pensacola. It's a good assumption. His grandfather had business and family connections in Mobile. The city

JAKE JACOBY

was a busy port and many immigrants arrived there, but right now we lack proof.

There is another possibility. The Sept. 1, 1904, *Canebrake Herald* (Uniontown, Ala.) mentioned Joseph Jacoby and noted he was a traveling salesman for his brother's business, Jacoby Grocery Co.. In the 1900 federal census, Jacoby lists his occupation as a salesman. Perhaps he traveled, and this photo might have been taken on a trip during the last years of the 1890s.

If we had the name of someone else in that group portrait we could use it to do additional research in passenger arrival records. The National Archives <**archives.gov**> has an Index to Passenger Lists of Vessels Arriving at Ports in Alabama, Florida, Georgia and South Carolina, 1890-1924 (T517). That missing piece of information could specifically date the photo and tell us its location.

Investigate the Caption

A caption runs along the bottom edge of the picture. Unfortunately, part of the cardboard is broken off, leaving us to guess at the rest of the information. I can't make out the first word, but there is a "....noon" or "roon" followed by "on board German Ship Baltimore." According to Jake Jacoby, below the caption and cut off in the scan of the photo is "Capt. Hillr..." The rest of his last name is missing.

When you're faced with incomplete caption information, it's best to start with what you know. In this instance,

CASE STUDY continued next page →

I did a Google search for *Ship Baltimore*. This search brought up a description of a German ship named *Baltimore* on **<theshipslist.com>**. It was built in 1868 for the North German Lloyd of Bremen and traveled from Bremen to Baltimore until 1872. In 1881, the ship was then used for service from Bremen to South America. However, this particular *Baltimore* was scrapped in 1894.

Another ship, the *City of Baltimore,* operated as part of the Baltimore Mail Line, but its dates of service are too late. It traveled from Baltimore to Hamburg in the 1930s. Not all information is online and I'm still looking for a good off-line resource for ship registrations. Consulting outside experts can often break the case so, I've spent hours calling folks knowledgeable about local history in both Mobile, Alabama and Pensacola, Florida, to learn more about the ship. No news yet, but perhaps some good leads on more family information for Jake to research.

Revisiting the Evidence

After another conversation with Jake, we came to the conclusion that his grandfather might not be greeting a group of immigrants. It could be another as-yet-unknown occasion. He doesn't think it's his grandparents' wedding because other family members aren't in the photo.

Listen to Readers

After my first blog post about this photo, I received comments about it from a couple of readers.

Genealogist Drew Smith, author of *Social Networking for Genealogists* (Genealogical Publishing Company) also did an internet search using the keywords *german ship baltimore.* His search turned up a mention of a German ship named *Baltimore* that sank on January 24, 1897, en route from London to New York. I followed this lead and discovered a couple of news stories. One was in the *New York Times* and the other is available through the Kentuckiana Digital Library's database of the *Daily Evening Bulletin* (Maysville, Ky.). Turns out that *Baltimore* was commanded by a Capt. Hillman, but as far as I know, it didn't carry passengers. It sank with its cargo of chalk aboard. However, I'm excited to find a possible name for the captain mentioned in the caption. The fifth letter of his name probably wasn't an *r*, but part of an *m*. We're hoping he commanded a different ship at some time prior to the sinking.

Another reader's great-grandfather was a ship's captain, and she still has his books. She checked in the *List of the Merchant Vessels in the United States, 1896* (p. 217) and found a yet another ship named the *Baltimore*. It appears to have been in Mobile, Alabama.

It's also possible that this vessel was a packet steam boat that operated between Mobile and Pensacola. Quite a few of them used Mobile as a port.

While this photo mystery is still a work in progress, we've been able to eliminate dead ends and get closer to the truth in this photo.

---

photographers did, but sometimes these props are distinctive. In one photograph I've seen, a woman held a picture of a fountain in her portrait. Her descendants are searching for the identity of the fountain, since it was obviously a picture of a place she once lived. Or you may have a photo of an ancestor holding a book written in another language—that provides a clue.

Some people even posed for portraits with the tools of their trade, such as a milkmaid who held her stool in one hand and a bucket in the other. While props can be mysterious, once researched, they can help you discover location and time frame for a picture.

Location

Outdoor pictures contain scenery, signage, and buildings, all of which can tell you about your ancestors. Even if the photograph was taken in the United States, immigrants often posed with clues to their heritage. In photos of individuals in front of buildings, analyze the architectural details that may reveal a specific regional or national style and time period. For a quick overview of foreign architectural styles, look at how immigrants influenced building in this country in *America's Architectural Roots: Ethnic Groups That Built America* edited by Dell Upton (New York: Preservation Press, 1995).

Celebration

Examine pictures of special events such as weddings, baptisms, and holiday celebrations for extra clues. Wedding traditions vary according to religious preference and cultural beliefs. Holiday decorations can tell you where the party was held or where a family's ethnic roots lie. Food can also tell you about your family: Each ethnic group serves particular food at special times.

COMPARING PICTURES

You probably know a little about your ethnic origins, so start with books that profile those groups in pictures, like the American Family Album series from Oxford University Press. The series features ten books with titles like *The Scandinavian American Family Album* and *The Mexican American Family Album*. Comparing your foreign photos with those in these books can help you make sense of mysterious details.

Search online bookstores for similar titles. Children's books like those in the *American Family Album* series contain a substantial number of illustrations for comparison.

Look at publications and Web sites generated by historical societies in areas settled by ethnic groups. The State Historical Society of Wisconsin published a series of short booklets on the various ethnic groups represented in their collection, complete with illustrations. Many other historical societies and libraries are digitizing their image collections. For example, the Minnesota Historical Society scanned the images in their photograph collection and posted them online. The largest digital database of pictures is the American Memory Project at the Library of Congress <**memory.loc.gov**>. For more Web sites with digitized images, see "Picturing the Past" by David Fryxell in *Family Tree Magazine* (October 2003).

Foreign picture mysteries are a little more challenging because the resources may be unfamiliar, but they are worth the extra effort. A single image can lead you to immigration documents and help you find the family members that stayed behind. An immigrant photograph visually connects you to your heritage.

FOLLOWING THE TRAIL

Besides using your photographs to identify where your ancestors came from, you can create a timeline of their lives in pictures. How? If you had an ancestor or group of relatives who traveled from their country of origin and then across the United States, you can track their movements through photographer's imprints. Families posed for pictures at several points in the Americanization and immigration process. They probably posed for a picture with family members before embarkation. One copy stayed with the nonimmigrants, and another accompanied those who left home. One of the first things families did once they were established in the United States was to have a family portrait taken, which they sent back to relatives who had stayed in the native land. In each new location, they posed for pictures and exchanged them with family overseas. By studying the photographer's imprint on each image in your collection, you can gather evidence on places they settled.

DOCUMENTARY EVIDENCE

After dating the photograph based on all the details present in the image, it's time to see if the evidence adds up to an identification. This involves re-examining your family history documents and looking for additional genealogical material, such as census enumerations, vital records, and immigration records. Photographs taken outside of the United States offer you an opportunity to connect with your ancestral roots in a foreign land if you pay attention to the details, research the facts, and add up the clues.

VAL FERNALD

The writing on the bottom of the photo on the left reveals that the image was taken by a photographer named Rossetti in Biella, an Italian town in the province of Novara. I couldn't find information about the photographer; however, the type of photograph helps to date the image. Along the bottom edge of the photograph appears the word *platinotipia*, which is Italian for *platinotype*, a type of paper print first introduced in the United States around 1880. The man's large mustache and loose-fitting coat and his wife's simple dress with slight pouching in the bodice date this image to about 1900.

The woman in this photo also appears in the family portrait on the right. She obviously links the families together—but who is she? Costume clues narrow the timeframe for these photographs. The dark clothing in the photo on the right is difficult to date, but the young mother's footwear stands out. Using John Peacock's *Fashion Accessories: The Complete 20th Century Sourcebook* (New York: Thames & Hudson, 2000), I was able to date these two-tone shoes to around 1929.

To identify foreign photographs, it's important to use resources such as family stories and immigration data in addition to photographic clues. These two pictures, taken approximately thirty years apart, only begin to tell the story of the Raiola family.

According to family lore, husband and wife Guglialmina Onesta (Honesta) and Ralph Raiola emigrated from Italy at different times. I searched for Ralph's name on Ancestry.com to see what genealogical data is available online. His name appeared in a California death record and two censuses.

Both the 1920 and 1930 censuses recorded the year of immigration. These documents show that Ralph immigrated to the United States in 1907 and had filed citizenship papers as of the 1930 census. At the age of

134

VAL FERNALD

digitized online, it's still worth a look at the microfilmed copies of the censuses to double-check data that's difficult to read online.)

Of course, in order to learn more about Ralph's time in the United States, the Raiola family should consult more resources than just these two censuses and the death record. One of the first rules of genealogical research is to work backwards, which means it's necessary to track Ralph's past in this country before trying to make the leap to Italy. Here are some steps for the family to consider, if they haven't already done so:

- Locate birth certificates for the two children and a marriage certificate for the couple.

- Look for Ralph's naturalization papers.

- Search for 1910 census data.

- Try to locate a 1907 passenger list for Ralph and a 1915 list for Guglialmina.

- This additional research can verify where in Italy the couple emigrated from, and it might supply other family names, as well.

- The photo on the left provides a starting place for foreign research: the Italian town of Biella. The older woman in both portraits could be Ralph's mother, the man in the photo on the left his father, and the child in that photo a sibling. When the photo on the right was taken, Ralph's father was deceased, and one of Ralph's siblings was married with children. It's possible that at least one of Ralph's siblings stayed behind in Italy to care for their parents. Additional research will help the family solve this photographic mystery. In fact, by searching Italian records, they may uncover a whole new chapter of Raiola family history.

twenty-seven, he married Guglialmina, also twenty-seven, who had immigrated to the United States in 1915. Ralph was thirty-one in 1920 and forty-one in 1930. By 1930, the couple had two children: Louis, fourteen, and Rosie J., nine, both born in California. The California Death Record lists Ralph's date of birth as 30 May 1888—only a one-year discrepancy from the ages recorded in the census. All this data suggests the couple married somewhere in the United States within a year or two of Guglialmina's emigration from Italy. (Even though the census sheets are

"Everybody, now-a-days, must have a Photograph Album, to be in fashion. It is an indispensable article for preserving the 'counterfeit presentment' of one's friends and constitutes one of the chief and most interesting ornaments of the parlor."

– "Photograph Albums," *Oregonian*, August 30, 1826.

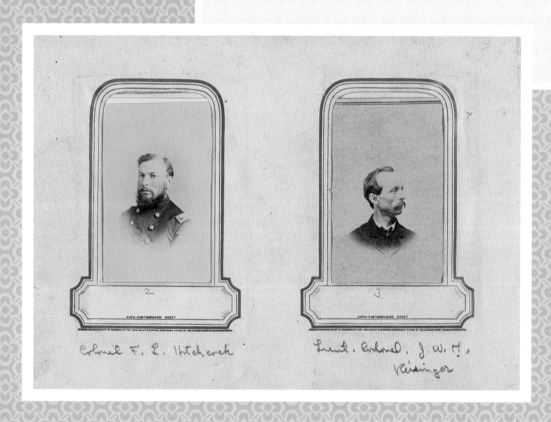

Colonel F. L. Hitchcock

Lieut. Colonel J. W. H. Reisinger

11

Photograph Albums

Do you own a photo album? That album tells a story. In most cases, the person who placed the images in the album arranged those images with a specific plan in mind. You can be sure that the person in the photo on the album's first page is very important to the creator of the album. It could be a child, a parent, or a spouse. Occasionally, it is a picture of the person who created the album.

1861
F.R. Grumel of Geneva, Switzerland, submits a patent in the United States for a photographic album (patent number 32,287).

1880s
Photo albums with plain paper pages become popular to hold candid photographs.

2004
According to the Photo Marketing Association, the average family photographer is a woman.

1880
The first mass-produced modern yearbooks appear with printed photographs or spaces for pasting in portraits.

1959
The National Union Catalog of Manuscript Collections (NUCMC) is established by the Library of Congress. It represents abstracts of manuscript and photo collections held in 1,300 different repositories.

Photo albums initially developed as a place where people could collect autographs or visiting cards of friends or famous individuals. Our ancestors arranged individuals—famous folks, friends, and family—in these albums. In some cases, photo albums represented interests, such as places visited, art pieces, or even scantily clad women.

The carte de visite created a new use for albums: Instead of collecting signatures, individuals could acquire photographs of visitors, friends, and celebrated persons. There were tiny, palm-sized albums for thumbnail-size tintypes, and for cabinet cards, there were large albums that resembled family bibles with velvet or leather covers and gilt edging.

These larger albums occupied a prominent place in households—on the corner table and in the parlor. Visitors added their images to them or gazed at the images already there.

The first albums were simple and copied designs available in Europe. On May 14, 1861, F.R. Grumel of Geneva, Switzerland submitted a patent in the United States for a photographic album (patent number 32,287). His design was for pages that allowed a single image or engraving to be inserted in each page. A mere year later, America was crazy for photograph albums. Initially high-priced, albums were imported from France and Germany, but it wasn't long before factories in the United States were producing photo albums. An article in the *Oregonian* proclaimed: "Everybody, now-a-days, must have a Photograph Album, to be in fashion. It is an indispensable article for preserving the 'counterfeit presentment' of one's friends and constitutes one of the chief and most interesting ornaments of the parlor. " They were available in a variety of retail outlets, including bookstores, as well as through mail-order.

Individuals began collecting photographs. For genealogists, a quote from the above article suggests we should look at our albums critically and carefully. "May it not be others, ny [sic] with many, as it was with a young person who lately showed us several pictures of young ladies. After looking at them and admiring them, we began to interrogate him whom they represented, and his reply from first to last was that he 'did not know.' "

The Civil War popularized photography and the use of albums to preserve and display these pictorial mementos. An 1864 article in the *Springfield* (Massa-chusetts) *Republican* proclaimed that "Civilians cherish them as among their dearest treasures and hardly a soldier goes forth to battle but carried one in his pocket, to be his shield, perhaps, in the hour of conflict, but at any rate his solace and delight in the monotony of the camp or on the lonesome and dangerous picket line." Advertisements suggested that every soldier should have an album. They could be ordered and mailed directly to them.

Small card albums held twelve images, while large albums held four on a page for a total of two hundred. In 1862, the American Photograph Albums manufactured by Samuel Bowles and Co. of Springfield, Massachusetts, cost between 75 cents to $6.50 depending on the type of album. This new industry added jobs and bolstered the northern economy.

Pictures were inserted in the cutouts provided in the albums. Card photographs inspired people, usually women, to create albums as memorials or as a form of entertainment. The rigid format of the albums didn't allow for much creativity.

Tintype albums offered the first departure from the traditional album. The thumbnail or gem-size pictures required a new format. Similar in design to the other books, gem albums fit in the palm of the hand and featured different styles of cutouts.

Albums with plain paper pages became available in the 1880s with the introduction of candid photography. No longer was the creator confined by the strict layout of the conventional album. Suddenly, albums fashioned by amateur photographers presented their personal view of the world in which they lived. The arrangement and placement of images tell us about the temperament and personality of the maker.

Albums featuring studio portraits were cooperative creations. The sitter posed for the camera, the photographer took the images, and the collector placed them in the album. Young women spent leisure time creatively laying out photographs in an expressive manner.

Candid photographs required a different type of album. Heavy sheets of black or white paper sewn together replaced the earlier formats. Individuals could lay out their images in any arrangement and add captions or scrapbook materials, such as newspaper clippings. Photographs could be cut into any shape and placed creatively in the album.

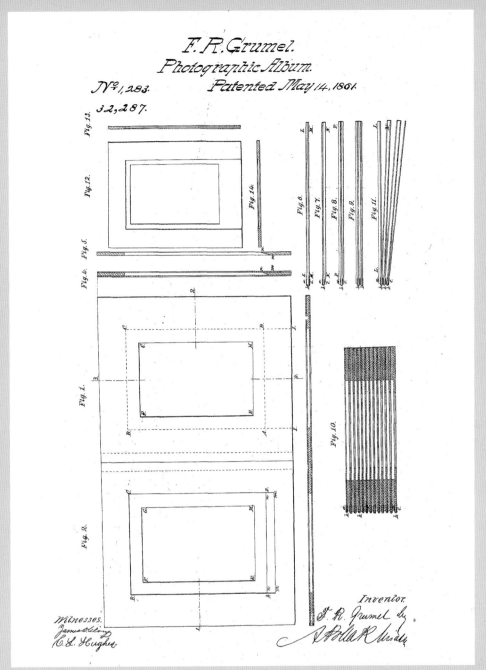

"Photographic Album," Patent Number 32,287. Filing date May 14, 1861. Invented by F.R. Grumel.

Snapshot photo albums offer insights into the world in which our ancestors lived. Individuals no longer needed to visit a studio to have a picture taken; this allowed amateur photographers to record their daily lives. People were no longer photographed just in their Sunday best, but in the process of work and play.

When examining the albums in your collection, pay attention to the individuals who are included, but use your genealogical research to notice who might be missing. Gaps in the photographic record might coincide with a tragedy or change in the family situation. You might discover that one album only depicts the college years of an ancestor, while another is an ongoing record of a life. Both men and women spent time creating albums or scrapbooks of their lives, but women were more likely to entertain themselves with these projects. John Hutchins Cady, a Brown University student in 1900, created a series of albums during his college years. He made his albums out of cloth and embroidered the edges with needlework before adding the images. His albums are a wonderful view of the life of a student at the beginning of the twentieth century.

I bought an album from the 1860s at an antique store and decided to see what I could learn about the family depicted in it. While many albums contain unidentified images, the owner of this one took time to label most of the pictures. However, these captions didn't always correspond to the photo inhabiting the slot. Older images had been replaced with newer ones. In other cases, the caption was all that remained.

The facts of this particular album are simple:

- There are twenty pages in the album with spaces for forty-two images.

- The leather cover features beautiful brass clasps.

- The photographs were taken between the early 1860s and circa 1870. There is a variety of cartes de visite images and a few tintypes.

- All of the images that have photographer's imprints were taken in Massachusetts.

Using genealogical databases, clothing details, and photographer's work dates, the story of this album was revealed.

Here are the first few pages from the album. I've listed the name of the person followed by details based on costume history, photographer's imprints, or genealogical data gleaned from the Web sites Genealogy Bank <**www. genealogybank.com**>, Ancestry.com <**ancestry.com**>, FamilySearch <**familysearch.org**> and Heritage Quest (a ProQuest database) <**www.heritagequestonline.com**>. Information on the photographers appeared in Chris Steele and Ron Polito's book *A Directory of Massachusetts Photographers 1839-1900* (Picton Press, 1993). Steele did extensive research using city directories and newspapers. Each piece of evidence helps tell the story of the album and the people depicted.

The 1850 U.S. Census for Cambridge, Massachusetts, lists the following household: Levi Hawkes (age 38), Caira Hawkes (age 40), Ellen E. Hawkes (age 13), Levi Hawkes (age 11), William H. Hawkes (age 6) and a Ward E. Hawkes (age 5) along with several other individuals. The father is a tin plate maker with real estate of $3,000.

The first page of the album features Ellen E. Hawkes. This image does not contain a photographer's imprint. The following costume details suggest this photo was taking in the early 1860s:

1. *large epaulets*

2. *small collar*

3. *belted waist*

4. *hair worn in side braids*

William Hawkes.   *Ward W. Hawkes.*

COLLECTION OF THE AUTHOR

Page two shows William Hawkes. According to the photographer's imprint, this slightly orange card photo was taken by Edward S. Dunshee who was at 3 Tremont St. in Boston from 1868–1887. This image was likely taken in circa 1870.

The third page contains an image of Ward W. Hawkes. According to the photographer's imprint, the studio of Harley & Metcalf's in Cambridgeport, Massachusetts, took this portrait. They were in partnership in 1860–61, so it's easy to

date this photo. Research on genealogy databases indicates Ward would be approximately age 15 at the time.

The fifth page contains a caption "Levi Hawkes" but the image is missing. An obituary for Levi Hawkes appears in the December 28, 1906, Boston Journal. He was remembered as one of the last survivors of Company C First Massachusetts Volunteers, a Civil War unit. But did the missing image depict the father or the son of the same name? Unless that missing image is located, the mystery will continue.

The first photo in the album depicts Caira and Levi's only daughter followed by the two youngest sons and their eldest, Levi.

Other Clues

Also depicted in the album on facing pages are Royal and Mrs. Sarah Douglas. Between them was a piece of red taffeta with hand-painted daisies. Albums were often used to keep mementos, but the meaning of this fabric is now lost.

On <familysearch.org>, a marriage record appears for Royal Douglas (one s) in Massachusetts Marriages, 1695-1910. He married Sarah F. Pond on April 3, 1840. The couple is included in single portraits in the album. In the 1870 U.S. Census for Cambridge, Royal lists real estate worth $10,000 and a personal estate of $1500.

The final image in the album depicts a group of five girls "from the Home for Little Wanderers." From their attire it appears the photograph was taken circa 1870. The photographer's imprint is for James W. Turner, at 47 Hanover St. in that period. Ten leading men from Boston established The Home for Little Wanderers in 1865 to care for Civil War orphans until they could be placed in other homes. The significance of this picture in the album is currently unknown.

Almost every album is a complicated collection of family, friends, and famous folks. In this case, research in vital records, newspapers, and census documents answered some of the questions.

CASE STUDY continued next page →

COLLECTION OF THE AUTHOR

Page six is an image of Mrs. Caira Hawkes. According to the photographer's imprint, J.W. Turner took this portrait of her. He was at 47 Hanover St. from 1860 to 1878. Her ruffled bodice suggests a date of circa 1870s. However, she still wears her hair in the style of the 1840s—looped with a bun in the back.

Page seven features Mrs. Adeline M. Douglass. This portrait was taken by Warren, who had offices in Cambridgeport and Lowell, Massachusetts. Dating it can be a bit tricky for a few reasons:

1. Her hair is in the style of the 1840s.

2. The wide lace collar is more appropriate for the 1850s.

3. Cameo-style portraits were popular in the early 1860s.

Information about the photograph helps clear up the confusion. Warren was at 100 Merrimack St. in Lowell from 1858–1861, so it's possible that this is a very early carte de visite.

In the 1850 census for Cambridge, Massachusetts, the 36-year-old Mrs. Adeline M. Douglass appeared living with her husband Robert (age 42), an Adeline Young (age 10) and a Mary Morgan (age 22). At the time, Robert was a Confectionary Manufacturer with real estate worth $37,000.

Who Created the Album?

From the evidence in the album layout and the genealogical clues, it seems likely that Caira Hawkes created the album. The fact that she placed her children first is a clue. Based on the dates for the images and the design of the album, she probably arranged the pictures in the early 1870s.

While the initial images depicted members of the Hawke family, there were several photos of the Douglas family. Further genealogical research made the link between the Hawkes and the Douglas families clear. According to the Massachusetts Deaths and Burials, 1795-1910, found on **<familysearch.org>**, Caira Hawkes was the daughter of Robert and Betsy Douglas. She was born in 1808 and died on August 3, 1877.

Obviously, there is a lot more research to be done to complete this pictorial family tree.

COLLECTION OF THE AUTHOR

Pages eight and nine contain images of James W. Greenwood. According the photographer's imprint, the image on the left was taken by Black & Batchelder, who were in business in 1860–61.

In the image on the right, Greenwood posed for William S. Warren in his Boston studio on 41 Winter Street. Warren was at this address from 1870 to 1888.

Greenwood aged considerably between the two portraits. The latter was likely taken in the 1870s. His obituary appears in the May 16, 1877 issue of the Boston Journal.

Greenwood appears in the 1872 Boston City Directory, found online at Damrell's Fire <www.damrellsfire.com>. According to the directory, he was a physician with an office at 13 Tremont Temple and a house at Cambridgeport, Massachusetts.

I'm unsure if James Greenwood was a friend, a member of the family, or a collectible image of someone famous.

"Success: The attainment of an object according to one's desire"

– OXFORD ENGLISH DICTIONARY

12

Adding Up the Clues

Do you believe that one photograph can really help you with your family history? For all the skeptics out there, the answer is yes. The basic tips are essentially the same as doing genealogy: Talk with relatives, do your research, and use online resources.

1973
The Internet is developed by American computer scientist Vinton Cerf as part of a project sponsored by the United States Department of Defense.

1991
Kodak makes photo CDs available.

2011
We are What We Do, launches Historypin.com, an interactive site where users pin their pictures to a virtual map and tell the story of the image.

1989
The World Wide Web is developed by English computer scientist Timothy Berners-Lee.

2001
Joe Bott launches the free photo reunion site DeadFred. com; the archive now contains more than 11,500 surnames and 46,700 photos.

For more than ten years, countless individuals have submitted historical images for identification in my Photo Detective columns that appear in Family Tree Magazine and online at <**blog.familytreemagazine.com/ photodetectiveblog**>. Incredibly, even after all this time, pictures continue to pour into my inbox. It seems that there is at least one picture mystery in every family. It's been an amazing journey. Here are some of cases I've investigated over the years and the ten clues that really work to resolve your picture problems.

> ### WHAT TO LOOK AT FIRST?
>
> When you have a mystery photo, try one of the following starting places and see if it leads you to an answer.
>
> - Family. What do you (or other relatives) know about the people in a picture? Listen to the photo's story and verify any facts you hear.
>
> - Photographic Format. Use the clues in the previous chapters to determine if you're holding an 1840s daguerreotype or a circa 1900 cabinet card.
>
> - Props. These can be difficult or impossible to identify, but they typically played an important role in an ancestor's life. They may be related to a profession, a club, or a family tradition.
>
> - Fashion Clues. Those head-to-toe clues can date a picture, but can also reveal ancestral interests and their fashion sense.
>
> - Photographers. A picture with the name or mark of a photographer is a genealogical gift. Research those photographers to determine the time frame in which the picture was taken.
>
> - Family History. Collect clues, research the evidence, and then compare the details to your assumptions about who's in the picture. If the facts don't add up, start over to see what you missed or re-examine your family tree for other possible matchups.

FAMILY FIRST

My very first online column featured a photo that's become symbolic of the type of questions I receive. Jackie Hufschmidt sent in a simple image of a couple taken in Eau Claire, Wisconsin. Hufschmidt didn't know the names of the people in the photo and couldn't imagine what her family was doing in Wisconsin. Shortly after the photo appeared online, several people wrote in to say that they either owned the same picture or that the photo looked familiar. A flurry of e-mails between these folks and Hufschmidt didn't reveal the reason behind this coincidental ownership. The final answer took several years and it was the result of talking with family. One of Hufschmidt's cousins happened to mention that she knew sisters who had moved to Eau Claire. It was a eureka moment for Hufschmidt. She rushed home and dug out another picture of the couple, surrounded by their kids, taken about twenty years after the original portrait. Patience and persistence paid off. You can read the full story in chapter two. When you have a mystery photo, show it to all of your family members. You never know who will have more information to help fill in the past.

FORMAT FOCUS

As regular readers know, not all mysteries are solved. It's a process of adding up the clues. A good place to start, after talking with family about curious pictures, is to look closely at your images and try to identify the photographic format. The format could provide you with a shortcut to a date range. The earliest type of photographic image, the daguerreotype, was on a shiny reflective metal surface. You must hold daguerreotypes at a 45 degree angle in order to view the image. Daguerreotypes were in vogue for about twenty years, a brief period compared to the longevity of another type of metal image— the tintype.

Patented in 1856, those tin (actually iron) pictures remained popular into the twentieth century.

Paper prints remain fashionable from the time of their introduction in the mid-nineteenth century to the digital craze of today.

Charles Blyth found this gorgeous daguerreotype in a group of identified family photographs and wondered if it depicted his great-uncle, Henry Blyth or a colleague of his. The fact that it was a daguerreotype helped determine that it could be either man. Henry

CHARLES BLYTH

The man depicted in this daguerreotype is holding a Wye level. The prop, the photography method and the age of the man in the photo suggest this could be Henry Blyth. Comparing the reverse daguerreotype to a known photo of Blyth confirms the identity.

CHARLES BLYTH

This is a photo of Henry Blyth taken in 1858.

Blyth was born in 1831, and the photographic method combined with his clothing style and age suggested it could be a photo of him in his twenties. An additional photo of Blyth taken in 1858 further convinced me that he was the man in the daguerreotype, as I explain in my July 8, 2008 Photo Detective blog post. To compare the two images required reversing the daguerreotype. Daguerreotypes are mirror-images of the scene captured on the silver plate.

Perfect Props

There was another piece of evidence depicted in Blyth's portrait—a piece of surveying equipment. I identified it as a Wye level used for long-distance surveying. Blyth was a surveyor in New York State before leaving home for Chile in 1853. This family data narrows the time frame for the daguerreotype. If, in fact, it's Blyth, then it was likely taken before he left for South America.

In the beginning, communication between me and readers was strictly via e-mail, but that changed in 2007 when the blog format was introduced. Now anyone can comment on the images featured in the online column. In fact, several people added their thoughts to the Blyth mystery including one woman who showed the column to her brother who is a surveyor. He told her that the item was, in fact, a Wye level and that "these levels were made so that the telescope could be taken out of its mounts and turned 180 degrees and remounted to be able to check the level bubble and cross hair adjustments while in the field." It was proof that an object held in a photo is more than a decorative device used by a photographer to add interest to a picture, it can actually deepen the photographic story.

BILL DODGE

The sleeves on these young ladies' dresses help date this photo to c. 1897.

ANCESTRAL FASHIONISTAS

When little is known about a photo, another a good identification rule is to start with what the people in the photo are wearing. There are elements of a person's dress that specifically date an image and details that reveal place of origin. Pay attention to every facet of style from head to toe. For instance, Bill Dodge asked me if one of the young women in this photo could be his paternal grandmother. He found the picture in his father's belongings. Each woman dressed in one of her best dresses. The women's attire sets the image in a specific time frame. It's relatively easy to tell when that was because all of them wear sleeve styles common in the 1890s. In my October 2, 2007 Photo Detective blog post, I dated this picture to about 1897. That's when tight lower sleeves accented by puffy upper sleeves started to become fashionable, yet you still see evidence of an earlier style. The two girls on the right in the back row wear the full sleeves popular from 1893 to 1896.

Dodge also wondered if it's a graduation photo, and if the girl on the lower right is holding a nurse's cap. The dress on the young woman on the lower right features an uncomfortable-looking, high-starched collar and attached scarf. It's actually the extra cloth on the scarf that resembles the shape of a nurse's cap. The fact that it's a group of young women all in their teens suggests that it could be graduation picture, just not one from a nursing school. A nursing school photo would fea-tures all of the girls posed in uniforms with caps on their heads. In the late nineteenth century (and even in many cases today) nursing schools had distinctive caps so that you could tell at a glance where they received their train-ing. As to whether or not one of the girls is his paternal grandmother requires comparing their faces to other images of the grandmother.

Clothing differences can be subtle or dramatic. It's a case of the more you look, the more you see. Take, for example, the photo of two women in unusual hats featured in the February 2007 Photo Detective column "Ancestral Wear-abouts" in *Family Tree Magazine*. It set the record straight on a myth regarding immigrant photos. First, everyday clothing depended on your ancestors' country of origin and where they lived (city or countryside), yet urban dwellers often wore current fashion popular in cities throughout Europe and the United States. Finding a photograph of an ancestor in interesting garb can reveal the ancestor's origins.

Odd clothing (like these women's hats) requires a special costume guide. Auguste Racinete's *Le Costume Historique*, first published in 1888 (reprinted in English in 2003 by Taschen), is expensive but useful, so try to locate it in a library collection. It covers the entire his-tory of costume, most of which pre-dates photography, but the final chapter is a genealogical gem full of color plates illustrating traditional fashion up to 1800. A much smaller book is Robert Harrold's *Folk Costumes of the*

World. His section on Wales contains a description on the history of that country's national attire. (If your photo lacks a photographer's name and you lack any knowledge of ancestral homelands, browsing these volumes looking for similar costume features may result in a match.) According to Harrold, a typical outfit consisted of a tall black beaver hat with white frilled bonnet, white blouse with red trim at the cuffs, a bright red underskirt, a checked apron and a shawl. These women lack the bonnet, white blouse and folded back skirt, but one wears the checked apron. Both wear the shawl and hat over ordinary everyday clothes.

These women's unusual hats were traditional attire in Wales. The Holyhead imprint confirms the photo is from Wales, as Holyhead is an island off the coast of Wales.

FAMILY COMPLEXITIES

Sometimes, it's the seemingly simple-looking pictures that cause the most trouble. Debbie Deaton sent me the lovely family portrait on page 150 hoping I could confirm the subjects' identities. This mystery made my eyes hurt and gave the owner a headache. She thought this portrait depicted the Deaton family: Franklin Deaton, his wife, Mahalia Mae Archer Deaton, and their children. Standing next to Mahalia is her son and Franklin's step-son, Harley. The other boy is Arthur Lee Deaton, the grandfather of Debbie's husband. The girl is supposedly Zelda.

First, I examined the clothing, but it didn't tell the whole story. The full sleeves on the women's dresses suggested a time frame of the mid-1890s. That's was the easy part. Regular readers know my mantra, "costume is only one clue." In the case of this picture, the family stories and genealogical researched solved the mystery.

When Debbie sent in the picture, she knew little about the individuals who posed for it. They lived in Oklahoma, and Mahalia was supposedly a full-blood Cherokee Indian. Franklin worked as a Sheriff. He died delivering a tax bill; as Franklin got to the door, the man who lived there shot Franklin dead.

I searched Genealogy Bank <**www.genealogybank. com**> for newspaper stories relating to Franklin, but didn't have any luck. Then I tried the Oklahoma Historical Society Web site <**www.okhistory.org**>, where you can search citations for Oklahoma newspaper articles. Unfortunately, Franklin didn't appear in the index. Digging a bit further, I decided to search the Federal Census using HeritageQuest Online (available through public libraries). I didn't find Franklin, but there was a 1900 census record for Mahalia. She was living with an Archer family. Her relationship to the head of the household is "step daughter;" Mahalia's children are "step grandchildren." Both Arthur and Zildy (Zelda) appear, but no Harley. This information confused the matter. If this picture showed Arthur (b. August 1894) and Zildy (b. January 1900), it certainly wasn't taken in the mid- 1890s. The children were too old and their ages reversed. The girl in this photo is older than both boys.

Instead of depicting Mahalia and her husband, could this image feature the Archer family from the census: Earl, his wife, their daughter and two youngest sons? Could this be a different husband? With questions racing through my mind and a deadline looming, I

DEBBIE DEATON

Though the females wear fashion from the 1890s, genealogical research dates this photo between 1902 and 1909. Use birth and death dates in combination with costume to date photos and confirm identities.

published the incomplete story in the Photo Detective blog on January 28. 2008.

Once again an astute reader found additional information. Turns out the answers were on the Pottawatomie County Genealogy Web site **<www.okgenweb. org/~okpottaw>**. Mahalia did marry another time. On May 13, 1902, Mrs. Mahalia Deaton married a George M. Crow in Pottawatomie County, Oklahoma. In the 1910 Federal Census for Ed Archer there are two Crow step-grandchildren, Harley and Jesse.

The reader suggested that the picture depicts Mahalia, George, Harley, Jesse, and Zelda Deaton. That's a likely scenario and, if it's true, means this photo was taken between 1902 (when she married George) and 1909 when she died. Her clothing is a little old-fashioned for the timeframe.

DON'T JUMP TO CONCLUSIONS

One of the most viewed Photo Detective blog posts is from October 13, 2008. It's a postcard with an intriguing image of four men, two of which are wearing only one glove. Sue Stevenson sent me the picture with a tentative identification. The man seated on the left is supposed to be Lance Melson (1907-1988) and the man seated on the right is supposedly Elmore Melson (1896-1938).

This single picture epitomizes my other mantra, "It's all about adding up the clues." Family history, general knowledge, photo format, and clothing all expanded what was known about this picture. There was so much

detail and material to cover that it became a serial of four separate blog posts. It was a layered tale with all the twists and turns of a good yarn.

This picture is a good example of how you need to question everything you find instead of jumping to conclusions. Let the scientific method rule your process. Follow the clues and see what they tell you rather than trying to make the elements fit an incorrect caption or family member's identification. Here's how the story unfolded.

Follow the Facts

I started by establishing the facts on this image. It's a real-photo postcard—a photograph with a postcard back. Turning over pictures is a must. There are often clues on the back. In this case, the format meant the picture was from after 1900, when the first real-photo postcards were introduced, while the particular stamp box design was common from 1904 to 1918. As I noted online, if this picture was taken in 1904, then one of the men couldn't be Lance Melson, who was born in 1908. Was it a case of mistaken identity?

Throughout the identification process, you'll ask questions, research clues, and even doubt your sources. The facts and family information in the Stevenson case simply didn't add up. When stumped, try another tact.

Look to the Clothing

The next step was to examine the men's clothing from head to toe. Their attire is a bit odd. Are their pants legs rolled up, or do they just have very wide cuffs? Cuffed pants were common on casual clothes in the early twentieth century, but the cuffs on these pants are a bit extreme. Neckties are the other interesting clothing detail. The man on the right in the front row wears a soft polka dot tie, a pattern that first appeared in the late nineteenth century.

As you examine clothing in your images, watch for unusual details, such as the one glove. It's curious that one man wears a glove on his right hand and the other on his left. I immediately thought, *Could this indicate their dominant hands and that the men wore them for work?* Stevenson was immensely curious about the glove and so were our readers. The second blog post focused on readers' theories including the possibility of artificial limbs.

SUE STEVENSON

This real-photo postcard presented a mystery solved by genealogy research and family stories

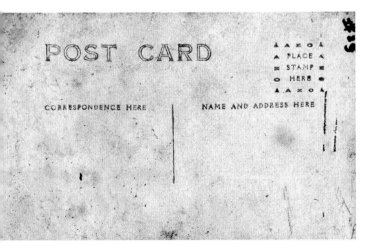

SUE STEVENSON

The reverse of this real-photo postcard dates the image to between 1904 and 1918.

Find a Look-a-Like

In the end, Stevenson discovered her older relatives had slightly misidentified the men. The relatives had said the two men in front were Melsons and the men in back were Wingfields. They were actually partially right. Comparing images of other family members in both families revealed distinctive physical traits. The Melsons have prominent ears, and these can be used as an identification clue. Features, such ears, noses, eyes and mouths, are quite useful for comparison. The men in the front row were Melsons. One could be Elmore, but Lance Melson could not be one of them.

Tree Trimming

Still armed with only definite dates relating to format and design, it was back to genealogical data.

Elmore Melson (b. 1896) had two other brothers: Joel (b.1894) and Bertram (b. 1892). Sue's family was partially right again. Lance Melson would be too young to be in the group photo, but Joel is old enough. He is the man seated on the right. His presence help specifically date the image and solve the one glove detail.

Putting it All Together

Here's how it all fit together. Family research revealed that Joel died of pneumonia in 1918 in Oklahoma, meaning the group portrait was likely the last image taken of him. He probably posed with his 22-year-old brother Elmore.

According to family stories, Joel Melson and his brothers worked as farmers and weren't very well-off. In Joel's spare time, he also worked as a bronco rider. My suspicion that the gloves were work-related was right. A bronco rider wears a glove only on his dominant hand.

The confusing clothing clues were also solved. The men's ties are Western in style. The suits, combined with the gloves, suggest this image commemorates a special event, such as winning a rodeo. And what about the cuffs? Once again, family stories illuminated a puzzling detail. Turns out that Joel wasn't very tall and instead of having his pants hemmed, he just rolled them up.

Not long after the third installment, a woman, Denise Damm, wrote to me about the men in the picture. The Wingfields (in the back row) were her relatives and she had pictures to prove it. It was an online reunion. The Melsons and Wingfields were cousins, but Stevenson and Damm didn't know each other.

Adah (Whitaker) Brown, her daughter, Gerzella, and her sister, Dessa Whitaker

RITA WERNER

Rita Werner identified these woman by connecting with a relative.

Rita Werner owned a photograph of three unidentified women that had plagued her for many years. Through a relative, she eventually found another picture that confirmed their identities. Her dad's cousin sent her photographs of her grandfather's family from the early 1900s, and she recognized one of the women immediately because of her tiny waist. These new photographs led to an exciting identification.

"The women are from my grandfather's side—not my grandmother's, as I had suspected. The woman on the left is my great-grandma, Adah (Whitaker) Brown, born in 1880. The woman on the right is her sister, Dessa Mae Whitaker, born in 1885. The child is my Grandpa Brown's only sister and my great-aunt, Dessa Mary Gerzella (possibly Grayzel) Brown. Now when I look at her with fresh eyes, I can see the resemblance to my grandpa! Gerzella was born in 1904. So now I know that it's Gerzella holding onto her mother and aunt's hands."

PHOTO REUNION SITES

In the last few years, the online community has developed a way to locate "missing" family photographs. Joe Bott of DeadFred.com <**www.deadfred.com**> and Daniel Pina of Ancient Faces <**www.ancientfaces.com**> have Web sites dedicated to reuniting people with their lost pictures. Initially, Joe only posted images from his own collection, but readers asked if they could upload their own "mystery images." The result is Dead Fred's online photo reunion site. Over twenty thousand people a day visit the site. One woman wrote to him about a photograph of a young couple in Texas taken in the 1890s—the picture was of her great-grandparents, whose faces she had never seen. Just in case other relatives are out there looking for the same pictures, Joe requires proof of the relationship and a waiting period before reuniting the photos with their families. To this date, he's reunited over two hundred photographs with their families.

ONLINE SUCCESS

The Internet also connects us to family photographs in collections around the world. A woman in New Zealand contacted Lindsay Lloyd in England to find out if Lindsay might be interested in an old photo album. By some unbelievable chance, it turned out the woman was related through Lindsay's husband's great-great-great-grandparents, who had immigrated to New Zea-

land. Lindsay verified the relationship by using the 1881 census for England and sorting out the identities of the people in the album. There was one unusual name that she recognized. Lindsay was astounded. She had no idea how they fit into the family. "Apparently he [the man with the unusual name] had been a godfather to her great-great-grandfather. These very same people had also owned our house when it was first built 150 years before. We had no idea of a family connection when we bought it, but now a photo of the original owner is hanging there!"

The Web attracts a huge audience and, since the first rule of photo identification is to show the mystery photo to relatives, why not place it online and hope that distant cousins can help you in the process? That's exactly what Sharon McKenzie did with images from her maternal grandmother's photo albums. Sharon and her mother had identified all but seventy of the photos. She scanned them and placed the images online, posting information about them on Rootsweb <**www.rootsweb.ancestry. com**>. One of the images was of an unidentified store. Sharon knew it must have been somewhere in Nebraska, probably dating from the late 1800s or early 1900s. She soon received a note identifying the town as Glenvil, Nebraska, and information on who owned the store, when the business was established, and even details on the first item sold. All this data came from someone

Chaplain Robert Stroud decided to investigate his wife's great-great-great-grandfather, John Moore, after finding an image of him dressed in the uniform of the Grand Army of the Republic (GAR), a Civil War veterans' group.

Robert knew that researching John Moore would be difficult, especially after he found more than eight hundred men of the same name in the Union army. Using the American Civil War Research Database available at <www.civilwardata.com> Stroud narrowed the list down to a much smaller pool of veterans who were from Iowa, survived the war, and had the same or no middle initial. Then, a relative saved Stroud from having to review all the records one at a time when he mentioning he owned some old documents. One of them happened to be John Moore's discharge papers, which had lain undisturbed in a drawer for more than a century. The correct John Moore was finally found.

As Robert discovered, talking about your research with other relatives can uncover new information, documents, and even photographs.

More Success

Robert Stroud continues to find new photographs to add to his collection. "One of the greatest joys in hosting a Civil War regimental Web site," he says, "has been making information available to the descendants of veterans which they would never have had access to otherwise. About a year ago, I was contacted by the great-grandson of one of the regiment's officers who was in the possession of his ancestor's wartime diary. What a priceless treasure! He made some of the diary available via the Fifth Iowa Volunteer Cavalry Web site. He mentioned the fact that his great-grandfather had also had a photo album that included images of thirty or forty soldiers, which had disappeared over the years. He recalled looking through the historic collection with his grandmother, and mourned its disappearance. By extension, I too regretted its loss, since his ancestor served in the same Company in which my great-grandfather was a noncommissioned officer. I thought that a picture of my own ancestor could well have been included in that very album, and that would be a wonderful discovery—not only for my immediate family, but for distant cousins with whom I have only become acquainted via the Web site.

"After corresponding for nearly a year with this man, I received an e-mail from another regimental descendant. He asked me to put him in touch with the diary owner, as he suspected they were cousins—he 'had in his possession the Company photo album belonging to his great-grandfather.' Needless to say, these two branches of an American family were reunited. And as if that was not rewarding enough for me … yes, you guessed it, the album did include a photograph of Corporal Chauncey William Stroud … and, if I might be so bold, I take pride in the fact that my forefather accented his military uniform with a stylish cravat when he sat for this studio photograph."

who wasn't a relative, but who knew the family and was able to put Sharon in touch with some distant cousins.

Not every family photo mystery can be resolved immediately. It takes time and patience to accumulate evidence, verify facts, and confirm assumptions. While the individuals featured in the case studies throughout this book have solved one photographic puzzle, they continue to search for new ways to date and identify the unknown images that remain in their collections.

A decade of researching images has taught me to never be surprised at the twists and turns in a picture quest. Truth is, you never know where your research is going to take you but, regardless, it's a fascinating journey. As I've learned, putting a name with a face is a lot of work that requires patience and perhaps eye drops (for the eye strain brought on by squinting at details). Whether you actually end up with a name or just a good story, it's important to remember that each and every picture has a story to tell. It's up to you to follow the clues to let the photo speak. Learn to read the visual clues present in every photograph—you never know when a single image will provide the answer to a genealogical brick wall. Dating and identifying family photos is challenging work, but it's never boring.

JANET MELENEY

So how long does it take to solve a photo mystery? In Janet Meleney's case it took nine years. In 2002, she submitted a lovely photograph to the Photo Detective online column. It depicted a large group of people standing on a wrought iron bridge. Meleney didn't know which side of her family was depicted in the photo or where it was taken. I was able to confirm the time frame for the image as the late 1860s.

I featured it in a short online piece in the hope that someone would recognize the bridge. Recently Meleney made a chance discovery in the New York Public Library digitized collections **<www.digitalgallery.nypl.org>** that helped her identify the bridge as the Loew Bridge, which stood over New York City's Broadway at Fulton Street for about two years—1866 to 1868.

The bridge's history is fascinating. Hatmaker John Genin advocated to the New York City Common Council that a bridge across the busy thoroughfare would increase the number of customers visiting his store. The bridge was constructed so that pedestrians could safely cross

Broadway and not risk death from horse-drawn vehicles. Two years later, rival hatmaker Charles Knox and his allies sued New York City for the removal of the bridge. Knox alleged the bridge adversely affected his business by causing his storefront to be in shadow.

The Loew Bridge was a famous span even memorialized in the poem "Loew's Bridge: A Broadway Idyl [sic]," by African-American poet Mary E. Tucker.

So often, a family photograph intersects with local or national history and those details help tell the story of a moment in time.

In this case, Meleney's picture represents a branch of her family as well as a "lost" piece of New York City history.

1. The bridge was built in 1866 as clearly marked on the side of the iron structure. The year is reversed, but that's not unusual in tintypes created in the 1860s. Reversal lens were available, but not all photographers used them.

2. Back in 2002, Meleney hoped the two little girls dressed in identical costumes in the left foreground were Carrie Ella Coit (1858-1934) and C. Miriam Coit (1856-1921). Behind the children is their mother, Ellen Nafie Coit (1827-1893). At the time, Meleney sent additional photographs for matching up facial features (eyes, noses, mouths, and facial shape) and I was able to use these to confirm the identities.

3. Dating the photograph was based on the ages of the girls and the clothing worn by the individuals in the picture. One fashion clue stood out. Black-and-white check prints (worn by a woman in the front row) were very popular circa 1868.

4. Since hatters were involved in the construction and demise of this structure, I can't help but wonder if the two men in the stovepipe hats in the back row bought their headgear at one of the nearby stores. By 1868, the stovepipe hat wasn't worn by every man. They were primarily worn by men in distinguished professions.

5. In 1868, most men favored the small-brimmed round hats like those worn by the man with the baby and the boys.

6. One of the outstanding questions about this photograph is who else posed for this shot. Are they all members of the Coit family or is this a group of spectators and family members? Watch for clusters of people in a large group picture. For instance, the woman in the checked dress and the man with a baby seem to be a family based on their proximity to one another. It appears to be a collection of family members, street urchins, and at least two well-dressed men of distinction.

7. I'm also interested in where the photographer stood to capture this picture. In a stereograph of the bridge found on Wikipedia, you can see the whole span. The photographer appears to have stood on the top landing of the staircase to capture the scene with the columned St. Paul's Church in the background. Search "Broadway Bridge Fulton St." in Google Images to see other views of this bridge.

Michael Hanrahan knows the identity of some of the women in this festive photo thanks to the inscription on the back: "Mom 2nd one on the right/1st on left Aunt Agnes Malcolm Riedy/ Left—4th Aunt Mary Collins Malcolm, 5th Aunt Minnie DeCory Malcolm, left center back Grandma Malcolm (Mary Moran Malcolm)." "Harry" is written above the name of Mary Collins Malcolm and "Bill" is written above Minnie DeCory Malcolm.

The inscription gives us a clue as to who labeled the picture—a child of "Mom" (Mae Malcolm Hanrahan) and grandchild of "Grandma Malcolm" (Mary Moran Malcolm). This photo was owned by Eileen C. Hanrahan Hourihan, daughter of Mary/Mae Malcolm and Charles Leo Hanrahan.

On the left is Mary Moran Malcolm. According to family information supplied by Michael Hanrahan and census data found on Heritage Quest (a ProQuest database) <heritagequestonline.org>, Mary Moran Malcolm was the wife of Andrew Malcolm and they had five children—Harry, Mary/Mae, Agnes, Margaret, and William.

Agnes Malcolm married Charles Riedy in November 1906. Harry Malcolm and Minnie DeCory married in August 1909, and William Malcolm married Mary Collins November 26, 1919, confirming that the "Harry" and "Bill" written above the women's names refer to their husbands. If Margaret Malcolm is in the photo, she is not identified.

Based on the clothing clues, this photo predates William's nuptials. The young women clustered around the table all wear various dress styles popular in the circa 1910 period. Some of the young women wear dresses of the pre-1910 period, while the young woman fourth from the right wears a dress from the early nineteen teens—round necklines and buttoned skirts. Mary Malcolm wears a hairstyle with a high topknot from the turn of the century. This picture illustrates that not every woman immediately followed the current fashion.

MICHAEL HANRAHAN

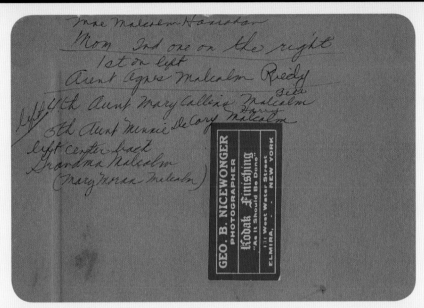

MICHAEL HANRAHAN

Mary/Mae Malcolm, married Charles Leo Hanrahan in 1914. This photo captures a group of young women at what is likely an engagement party for Mae. The presence of the crepe paper, the good crystal, and the cake suggest a special occasion. The marriage date helps to establish a time frame for this image—sometime before 1914—but because terms of engagements vary and the family doesn't know when the couple became betrothed, it's difficult to determine an exact date.

Study the arrangement of the women in this photo. The two eldest stand at the head of the table indicating they have coordinated the event. We know the woman on the left is Mary Moran Malcolm. The unidentified woman on the right is probably Charles Hanrahan's aunt, Charlotte "Lottie" Henderson, who moved in with the family to raise Charles and his two sisters, Eva (b. 1892) and Agnes (b. 1895), when their mother died in 1897. It's possible that Charles's sisters are also in the picture, perhaps the young women next to Lottie. One of the other unidentified women could be Mae's sister Margaret, something that could be determined by comparing another photo of her to the faces in this image.

The bride's parents usually hosted events like this, so this image gives the descendants a peek into their ancestral homestead at 329 Roe Ave, Elmira, New York. A search of early twentieth century insurance atlases at the local historical society could confirm the location.

There is more on the back than just the names. The photographer glued a business label to it: "Geo. B. Nicewonger, Photographer, 131 West Water Street, Elmira, New York." Nicewonger lists his occupation in the 1910 and 1920 census as a photographer. His obituary appeared in the Syracuse Herald Journal, August 17, 1946 (available on **<ancestry.com>**). For this photograph in a small dining room, he used a flash, but also illuminated the scene with the table lamp.

The ballpoint pen used to write the names wasn't sold until 1945, providing a beginning time frame for when Eileen labeled the image. See **<www.ideafinder.com/history/inventions/ballpen.htm>** for more on the history of the ballpoint pen.

GRANT EMISON

This photo mystery remains unsolved.

In the Emison/Loock family photo collection, there is a haunting image of two girls in plaid dresses. While their identities remain unknown, the true mystery is why they have bald heads and no eyebrows. Lynn Betlock has made several attempts to figure out who these mysterious girls in her husband's family are and the reason for their appearance. Sometimes, even with persistence and patience, images in your collection will defy your efforts to identify them.

The photograph is a carte de visite, a process introduced to the United States in 1859. The photographer's imprint on the reverse of the image is for Barr & Wright, which places the subjects in Houston, Texas, in the period from 1870 to 1879–80.

A costume historian verified that the girls' dresses place them within the 1870s. The historian also offered the hint that people who contracted yellow fever often lost their hair or had their heads shaved.

Library research confirms that there was a major yellow fever epidemic in Houston in 1867. In a town of less than 5,000 people, 492 died. By consulting the National Library of Medicine and the National Institute of Health's "History of Medicine" **<www.nlm.nih.gov>**, Lynn was able to learn that only one disease causes hair loss of the type depicted in the photograph—alopecia, a congenital condition that causes people to lose the hair on their bodies.

The Emison family is fairly well-documented in photographs from the first decade of the twentieth century to the present, but no photos in the family archive exist for the time period of the girls in the plaid dresses. There is no photographic evidence in the family collection to suggest that alopecia is present.

The photos in the Emison/Loock collection are primarily of the Loock side of the family, so they became the focus of the research. Lynn traced several family groups, but in each case the genealogical research did not establish an identity for the girls.

By comparing the family information with what is known about the image, Lynn considered the idea that the two girls were Mamie Evansich and her sister Lula. Research showed that they could not be the girls, however, because they weren't living in Houston in the 1870s. Both girls were born in Brenham, Texas, which is eighty miles from Houston. More important, Mamie and Lula were born too late to be possibilities.

Lynn then tried to locate other Loocks living in the area in the 1870s to see if there was a connection. In the 1870 census, she found another Loock family living in Houston. The daughters of Henrietta Loock Gastman and her husband Henry were approximately the right age. In the 1870 census, Henrietta and her husband are 25 and 30, respectively. They have three daughters: Dorothea, age 9; Anna, age 7; and Mary, age 4. Any two of these daughters could possibly be the girls in the photograph. Mary is known to have lived to adulthood, but nothing is known about the two other siblings. No relationship with the other Loock family in Brenham could be established. The families attended different churches and were not mentioned as baptismal sponsors or in obituaries.

Lynn also found Hermann Loock, who was born in Hanover, Germany, and was living in Houston in 1870. Once again, however, research showed that not only were his children born too late, they were both boys.

Another possibility is that the girls' photo found its way into the family collection through family friends. According to the 1870 Texas census, Hermann Loock was living with another family, the Kothmanns, as a boarder. The Kothmanns had two girls that were the right age, but there are no other images of them that could prove they are the mystery girls. There are also no death records for their daughters, so there is no evidence they were living between 1870 and 1879–80.

All the genealogical research implies that the girls were probably not related to the Loocks. The medical information concerning their lack of hair supports the genetic disease alopecia, but no other members of the Loock family have been known to have the disease.

Nineteenth-century families collected cartes de visite for a variety of reasons. Medical anomalies were photographed, and the images sold to collectors. It is possible that this image falls into that category and the image is not of anyone in the Loock or Kothmann families.

Appendices

LABELING YOUR IMAGES

WORKSHEETS & IMPORTANT ADDRESSES

LABELING YOUR IMAGES

As you identify your family photos, it is important to label each image. A worksheet is a useful tool, but if it becomes separated from the item, the information is lost. The best way to include identification data is to place the photograph in an archival sleeve with acid-free paper. Archival materials will not harm your images. You can then write the caption on the acid-free paper with a pencil. Archival-quality materials can be purchased in a local photography store or from a specialty supplier. Acid-free paper can be purchased at most office supply stores.

You can also create an album of your family images, as long as the materials you use are guaranteed safe for photographs. Albums that use static electricity, glue, or a plastic overlay to hold the images in place are not safe to use. It is best to purchase quality materials from one of the suppliers listed in the appendix.

Tools

Before you begin labeling photographs, there are a few precautions you need to take. First, don't write on the front of an image, because you don't want to mar the surface of your picture. Second, never use a ballpoint pen or a felt-tip marker. Ballpoint ink smudges and you can make indentations in the image, while the felt-tip marker's water-soluble ink can be absorbed by the picture.

There are two different types of writing implements that you can use for identification purposes. A soft lead pencil, like a graphite artist sketching pencil, is best for labeling paper photographs. A special pen is necessary to write on contemporary paper prints that are on RC (resin-coated) paper. Look for pens that advertise that their ink is waterproof, fade resistant, permanent, odorless (when dry), and quick drying. Black ink is preferable since colored inks tend to fade over time. Both of these implements are readily available in art supply and scrapbook stores.

Captions

The type of information you need to include in your caption/label is the same regardless of the type of photograph—full names and life dates. If you have a group portrait, try to name as many people as possible. Don't worry if you lack certain names, are uncertain of a woman's maiden name, or only know when someone died. Having partial information is better than having none at all. Record when or where a picture was taken, and if you know the occasion, include that as well.

INFORMATION TO INCLUDE IN PHOTO CAPTIONS

Person

- Full name

- Dates of birth and death

- Name of photographer

- Date image was taken

- Event depicted

- Original owner or citation of where the image was found, including page numbers

- Your name and the date you labeled the image

Place

- Geographic location

- Title of image (if not supplied, place in brackets)

- Photographer

- Date image was taken

- Original owner or citation of where the image was found, including page numbers

Labeling

Now that you know what information to include and have the tools you need, it's time to learn how to label all the different types of pictures found in your family photograph collection.

CASED IMAGES

You can't write directly on cased images, such as daguerreotypes, ambrotypes, and tintypes, but there are storage and labeling methods that work. Some people include small slips of acid- and lignin-free paper, but those have a tendency to get misplaced. The best way to label your cased images is to purchase small acid- and lignin-free envelopes or small boxes and write the identification on the storage container.

TINTYPES

These metal images are also found in paper mounts or without any enclosure. You could attach a label to the back of the image using adhesive, but I don't recommend affixing anything to your original images. Instead, place the tintype in a polypropylene or Mylar sleeve large enough to accommodate a piece of acid- and lignin-free paper behind the image. You can then write on the paper without causing damage to your heritage photograph. Polypropylene and Mylar products as well as acid- and lignin-free enclosures are available from the suppliers in the appendix.

PAPER IMAGES AND CONTEMPORARY PHOTOGRAPHS

Paper prints and resin-coated (RC) pictures are the easiest images to label, because you can write on the back or use the method suggested for tintypes. Using the appropriate tool, place the image facedown on a clean hard surface and gently write the identifying information.

SLIDES

Use a fine-point marker with the same specifications as those necessary for RC prints—waterproof, odorless (when dry), fade resistant, and quick drying. You can use this type of pen for both paper and plastic mounted slides.

DIGITAL IMAGES

It's never been easier to label your digital images. New software on the market for organizing digital photos allows you to caption your pictures using keywords. It will arrange images regardless of format or whether they were taken with a digital camera, downloaded, or scanned.

NEGATIVES

Polypropylene pages made for negative storage make finding your negatives a snap! Across the top of the page, include a brief description of what is on the roll and when the pictures were taken. Number each negative to correspond to its description. Try storing all your negatives in notebooks for easy retrieval.

A common problem is figuring out how to file negatives and cross-reference them with their prints. Since labels have a tendency to fall off as the adhesive ages, write the number of the negative in the bottom right corner on the back of each photo using a special marking pen. If you want to use labels, select those that use acid- and lignin-free paper and adhesives.

WORKSHEET: **CASED IMAGE**

Attach photocopy of image

TITLE/SUBJECT/CAPTION: ______________________

____

IDENTIFYING MARKS: ______________________

____

PHOTOGRAPHER'S NAME: ______________________

DATES OF OPERATION: ______________________

COLORING DETAILS: ______________________

____

COSTUME DESCRIPTION: ______________________

____

____

____

OTHER INFORMATION: ______________________

____

____

____

OWNER'S NAME: ______________________

ADDRESS: ______________________

____

____

TELEPHONE NUMBER: ______________________

CONDITION: ______________________

TYPE OF IMAGE: ______________________

TYPE OF CASE: ______________________

SIZE (H X W): ______________________

HINGES: ______________________

CASE MANUFACTURER: ______________________

DESCRIPTION OF CASE DESIGN: ______________________

____

PROPS AND BACKGROUND: ______________________

____

COSTUME TIMEFRAME: ______________________

Download a digital copy of this worksheet at **<familytreeuniversity.com/familyphotodetective>.**

Attach photocopy of image

TITLE/SUBJECT/CAPTION:

IDENTIFYING MARKS:

PHOTOGRAPHER'S NAME:

COLORING DETAILS:

COSTUME DESCRIPTION:

OTHER INFORMATION:

OWNER'S NAME:

ADDRESS:

TELEPHONE NUMBER:

CONDITION:

TYPE OF IMAGE: SIZE (H X W):

MOUNTED?   YES   NO   THICKNESS:

TYPE OF MOUNT:

ORIGINAL OR COPY?

PHOTOGRAPHER'S IMPRINT:

DATES OF OPERATION:

PROPS/BACKGROUND:

COSTUME TIMEFRAME:

WHEREABOUTS OF NEGATIVE:

WORKSHEET: **NEGATIVES**

Attach photocopy of image

TITLE/SUBJECT/CAPTION: ______________________

____

IDENTIFYING MARKS: ______________________

____

PHOTOGRAPHER'S NAME: ______________________

____

COLORING AND TOUCH-UP DETAILS: ______________________

____

COSTUME DESCRIPTION: ______________________

____

____

____

OTHER INFORMATION: ______________________

____

____

____

OWNER'S NAME: ______________________

ADDRESS: ______________________

____

____

TELEPHONE NUMBER: ______________________

CONDITION: ______________________

TYPE OF NEGATIVE: ______________________

SIZE: ______________________

SUPPORT MATERIAL: ______________________

APPROXIMATE DATE: ______________________

PHOTOGRAPHER'S IMPRINT: ______________________

PROPS AND BACKGROUND: ______________________

____

____

COSTUME TIMEFRAME: ______________________

DATE PRINT FROM NEGATIVE MADE: ______________________

Download a digital copy of this worksheet at **<familytreeuniversity.com/familyphotodetective>.**

WORKSHEET: **PRINTS (GROUP SHOTS)**

Attach photocopy of image

TITLE/SUBJECT/CAPTION: ______

______

IDENTIFYING MARKS: ______

______

PHOTOGRAPHER'S NAME: ______

______

COLORING DETAILS: ______

______

COSTUME DESCRIPTION: ______

______

______

______

OTHER INFORMATION: ______

______

______

______

OWNER'S NAME: ______

ADDRESS: ______

______

______

TELEPHONE NUMBER: ______

CONDITION: ______

TYPE OF IMAGE: ______ SIZE (H X W): ______

MOUNTED? YES NO ______ THICKNESS: ______

ORIGINAL OR COPY? ______

PHOTOGRAPHER'S IMPRINT: ______

DATES OF OPERATION: ______

PROPS/BACKGROUND: ______

______

COSTUME TIMEFRAME: ______

WHEREABOUTS OF NEGATIVE: ______

______

Download a digital copy of this worksheet at **<familytreeuniversity.com/familyphotodetective>**.

KEY TO WORKSHEETS

APPROXIMATE DATE OF NEGATIVE:
Based on the type of negative and the support material.

CASE MANUFACTURER:
Name of manufacturer.

CONDITION:
Assign a value (poor, fair, good, excellent) to the condition of the image, negative, or cased image. Describe any damage.

COLORING DETAILS:
Outline what parts of the image are colored.

COSTUME DESCRIPTION:
Using the charts in chapter nine, briefly describe what the individuals are wearing, including accessories.

COSTUME TIMEFRAME:
Assign dates to the costume styles.

DATES OF OPERATION:
Dates when the photographer was in business.

DATE PRINT FROM NEGATIVE MADE:
When a print was made from the negative.

DESCRIPTION OF CASE DESIGN:
Identify the key elements of the design.

HINGES:
Describe the type of hinges and clasp used on the case.

IDENTIFYING MARKS:
Make note of business cards on the back, patent notices, etc.

MOUNTED:
Yes or no.

ORIGINAL OR COPY PRINT:
Date of copy print if known.

OWNER'S NAME AND ADDRESS:
Be as complete as possible. Previous owners can be recorded on the back of the worksheet.

PHOTOGRAPHER'S IMPRINT:
Record type of imprint and the exact way it appears on the image.

PHOTOGRAPHER'S NAME:
Include this if known. This is different from photographer's imprint.

PROPS/BACKGROUND:
Describe the types of props and background used.

SIZE OF CASE:
Dimensions in inches.

SUPPORT MATERIAL FOR NEGATIVES:
Glass, paper, or film.

TITLE/SUBJECT/CAPTION:
Copy information as it appears on the image. Place handwritten captions in quotation marks. Titles you assign should be placed in brackets. Include life dates for the subject if known.

TYPE OF IMAGE:
Daguerreotype, Ambrotype, or Tintype, etc.

TYPE OF MOUNT:
What the photograph is attached to such as glass, board, or metal.

TYPE OF NEGATIVE:
Glass, paper, nitrate, or safety film.

TYPE OF CASE:
Wood, cardboard, leather, or union case.

WHEREABOUTS OF NEGATIVE:
Complete information on the owner of the negative if known.

IMPORTANT ADDRESSES

Conservators

AMERICAN INSTITUTE FOR CONSERVATION
OF HISTORIC & ARTISTIC WORK, INC. (AIC)
Conservation Services Referral System
1156 15th Street NW, Ste. 320
Washington, DC 20005
(202) 452-9545
info@conservation-us.org
<www.conservation-us.org>

CONSERVATION CENTER FOR ART
& HISTORIC ARTIFACTS (CCAHA)
264 South 23rd St.
Philadelphia, PA 19103
(215) 545-0613
ccaha@ccaha.org
<ccaha.org>

NORTHEAST DOCUMENT CONSERVATION
CENTER (NEDCC)
100 Brickstone Square
Andover, MA 01810
(978) 470-1010
<nedcc.org>

Societies and Organizations

DAGUERREIAN SOCIETY
PO Box #306
Cecil, PA 15321-0306
(412) 221-0306
<www.daguerre.org>

INTERNATIONAL KODAK HISTORICAL SOCIETY
P.O. Box 21
Flourtown, PA 19031
(215) 233-2032
<www.kodakhistoricalsociety.org>

INTERNATIONAL PHOTOGRAPHIC HISTORICAL
ORGANIZATION (INPHO)
P.O. Box 16074
San Francisco, CA 94116
(415) 681-4356
<www.well.com/user/silver>

NATIONAL STEREOSCOPIC ASSOCIATION (NSA)
<www.stereoworld.org>
strwld@teleport.com

PHOTOGRAPHIC HISTORICAL SOCIETY
250 Whiting Road
Webster, NY 14580
<http://people.rit.edu/andpph/tphs.html>

Suppliers

CONSERVATION RESOURCES
5532 Port Royal Road
Springfield, VA 22151
(800) 634-6932
<www.conservationresources.com>

GAYLORD BROS.
P.O. Box 4901
Syracuse, NY 13221-4901
(800) 962-9585
<www.gaylord.com>

HOLLINGER CORPORATION
9401 Northeast Drive
Fredericksburg, VA 22404
(800) 634-0491
<www.hollingermetaledge.com>

UNIVERSITY PRODUCTS
517 Main St.
P.O. Box 101
Holyoke, MA 01041-0101
(800) 628-1912
<www.universityproducts.com>

Index

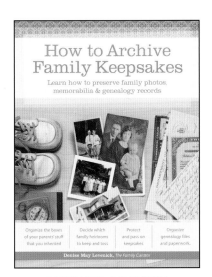
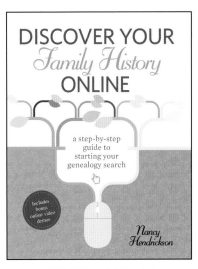
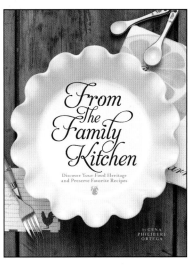

Looking for More Help
With your Family Photo Mysteries?

Check out these titles by Maureen A. Taylor.

Fashionable Folks: Bonnets and Hats 1840–1900

Fashionable Folks: Hairstyles 1840–1900

Finding the Civil War in Your Family Album

Preserving Your Family Photographs

Available from **<ShopFamilyTree.com>**.

ABOUT THE AUTHOR

Maureen A. Taylor is an internationally known photo identification expert and a genealogist. She travels extensively lecturing on photo identification, photo preservation and family history. She is a contributing editor to *Family Tree Magazine* and has written the Photo Detective blog since 2001. She is the author of *Preserving Your Family Photographs* and the *Last Muster: Images of the Revolutionary War Generation.* She has appeared on *The Today Show, The View,* and MSNBC. Her website is <**www.maureentaylor.com**>.

ACKNOWLEDGMENTS

It's been more than a decade since I wrote the first edition of this book, which was originally titled *Uncovering Your Ancestry Through Family Photographs,* for Family Tree Books. There are many people to thank for their encouragement and support in writing that book and updating the material for this revision under a new title—the *Family Photo Detective.*

It's amazing how many people around the world regularly read my online photo detective blog at <**www.familytreemagazine.com**> and submit their family photographs for identification. Their inquiries give me the opportunity to spend hours researching photo history, piecing together their picture puzzle. I've made many new friends while chatting with them via e-mail about their images.

I'm lucky to have friends like Lynn Betlock, David Lambert, Michele Leinaweaver, and Jane Schwerdtfeger who share my passion for old photographs. They also listen to my ideas and offer suggestions. Everyone should be so fortunate.

Several friends and colleagues read the original manuscript: Marcia Melnyk; David Mishkin of Just Black & White; Nancy Rexford; Alison Cywin formerly of-the Rhode Island Historical Society; and Jonathan Galli, CG. Other individuals acted as consultants on research problems, in particular Chris Steele and Jerome Anderson. Michele Leinaweaver and Betty Ann Tyson offered editorial advice.

New photo-related friends include Joe Bott of Dead Fred <**www.deadfred.com**>**,** Daniel Pina of Ancient Faces <**www.ancientfaces.com**>, Footnote Maven of Shades of the Departed <**www.shadesofthedeparted.com**>, and James Morley of <**www.whatsthatpicture.com**>**,** What's That Picture . We've become a community of folks passionate about pictures. The photo world changed with the introduction of social media—Flickr <**www.flickr.com**> and the new entries of Historypin.com <**www.historypin.com**> and 1000 Memories <**1000memories.com**> to name a few outside of the usual suspects of Twitter, Facebook, and Google+. I'm sure more exciting developments are in the future.

Editor Sharon DeBartolo Carmack introduced me to Betterway Books, now Family Tree Books, and guided me through the publication process for the first edition. Without her prodding, this book would not be a reality. Thanks also to Erin Nevius, David Fryxell, Susan Wenner Jackson, Allison Stacy, Diane Haddad, Jacqueline Musser, and Lauren Eisenstodt, current and past editors of *Family Tree Magazine*, for letting me write about what I love—family photographs.

Thank you to all of the individuals who contributed photos to this book. Their names appear in credit lines under the images. Some of the material presented here originally appeared in *Ancestry Magazine*, my "Photo Detective" column on the *Family Tree Magazine* Web site, or in *Family Tree Magazine.*

This book and my work with photographs resulted in some opportunities. In 2007, *The Wall Street Journal* acknowledged my passion for identifying family photographs with a two-page story in their *Weekend Journal*. A few months later I wrote about what may be the first American family photograph for the Smithsonian's site Click! Photography Changes Everything <**click.si.edu**>. Now that essay is part of a book edited by Marvin Heiferman, *Photography Changes Everything* (Aperture/Smithsonian, 2012).

A lot of people have written or spoken to me about how my work with photographs has helped their genealogical research and writing. I know that studying the relationship between photographs and family history has also changed my life.

Of course, no acknowledgment would be complete without mentioning my family. Thank you Dexter, James, and Sarah for understanding my obsession with history and photographs.